"Elohim Created"

A New Look at the First Creation Narrative

"Elohim Created"

A New Look at the First Creation Narrative

by

Richard H. Bulzacchelli

THE AGGIORNAMENTO PROJECT
NASHVILLE, TENNESSEE

"Elohim Created": A New Look at the First Creation Narrative

Copyright © 2012 by Richard H. Bulzacchelli

All rights reserved. With the exception of short excerpts for critical review, no part of this book may be reproduced or transmitted in any form or by any information storage or retrieval system, without permission in writing from the copyright holder or his executor. All quotations from Scripture, except where otherwise noted, are those of the author, and fall under this copyright notice.

ISBN: 978-0615745640

Nihil obstat: Sr. Mary Angelica Neenan, O.P., S.T.L., S.T.D.
       Censor Deputata

Imprimatur: ✠ Most Rev. David R. Choby, D.D., J.C.L.
       Bishop of Nashville

       December 7, 2012

The *Nihil obstat* and *Imprimatur* are official declarations that a book or pamphlet is free of doctrinal and moral error. No implication is contained therein that those who have granted the *Nihil obstat* and *Imprimatur* agree with the opinions expressed.

To Joseph Ratzinger / Pope Benedict XVI

On the Occasion of the Year of Faith

"When the question of the meaning of the first chapters of Genesis is posed on the terms of historicism, on the one hand, and of modern science, on the other, then this is a new question, for which no universal answer yet exists. . . . We must grope our way once more and go through it again."

—Joseph Ratzinger

TABLE OF

Contents

FOREWORD by Mike Aquilina 1

INTRODUCTION: Choosing between Two Worlds 4

CH 1: Babylonians in the Background 8

    After the Exile 9
    Paganism and the Cosmos 13
    Paganism and the Feminine 19
    The Babylonian Alternative? 31

CH 2: The Idea of Creation 35

CH 3: The Structure and Purpose of the Genesis Narrative 47

CH 4: A Theological Interpretation of the Genesis Narrative 53

Day One.. 54
Day Two 61
Day Three 64
Day Four 70
Day Five 76
Day Six 81
Day Seven 99

CH 5: The Genesis Narrative after the Fall of Babylon 107

The Woman and Her Seven Sons 110
Whither the Babylonians? 112
The Modern Areopagus 114
The Irony of Modernity 119
The Enduring Wisdom of the Dogma of Creation 121
Creation or Evolution? 123

APPENDIX: The Genesis Narrative in Translation............. 129

Foreword By

❦

Mike Aquilina

> *"Ezra read clearly from the book of the law of God, interpreting it so that all could understand what was read. . . . [and] all the people were weeping as they heard the words of the law."*
>
> — Nehemiah 8:8–9 (NAB)

We have lived so long with the story of our creation that we take it for granted. Its implications have become our cultural wallpaper, no longer seen—white noise, no longer heard. We have built a civilization upon its suppositions, which are the bedrock of our international treaties and national constitutions.

As westerners and as moderns, we hold certain truths to be self-evident: human dignity and equality, for example, human rights, and a common, universal human kinship. We desire world peace. We celebrate the order of the cosmos, which we observe and measure and exploit through our sciences and technology.

We assume, moreover, that all these principles and accomplishments were inevitable, just a gradual working-out of human nature. But that's not true to history.

Only with Judaism and Christianity—and their particular account of human origins—did human beings begin to dream of the possibility of world peace and common human rights. Until the rise of Christianity—with its idea of a rational God and an ordered creation—the empirical sciences were stillborn. Many great discoveries were made in China, India, and Mexico; but only in the Christian West did science become an unstoppable wave of one astonishing discovery after another.

The Babylonians could not have given us what we love about our world. The Greeks and Romans could not have given us the good things we now take for granted.

The Book of Genesis, with its unique account of creation, made our world possible. If we do not appreciate that fact, we do not know who we are. If we do not appreciate that fact, we understand little about our world.

Richard H. Bulzacchelli has taken the oldest story in the world and somehow made it new and fresh for us. How? He has taken us back to the great personalities who first wrestled with its meaning, and he has amplified their voices for a generation almost deaf to tradition.

Revolutions are made from books like this one. Read it, and see your world as something new—coming from the hand of God.

INTRODUCTION

Choosing between Two Worlds

Many people today think that they must choose between the Bible and scientific discovery. They think that if human beings evolved gradually from lower life forms, the Bible cannot be true, or that it cannot be true if the universe came into being from a "big bang" billions of years ago and gradually took the shape it has right now. Not only do people of faith often think this way; people without faith think this way as well. That fact has led to repeated conflicts in our public schools over whether and to what extent "alternative theories of origins" might be proposed in the classroom. Some think that such alternative theories of origins are necessary for the preservation of even the possibility of faith in the modern world, while others think it is nothing more than the invalidation of science in favor of fantasy.

Both sides of this debate are right, and both sides are wrong. The error comes in the form of a false dichotomy. By casting the problem in the way that we have, we draw a line in the sand that our interlocutor dare not cross except at the expense of his most principled beliefs. No person of good will could be expected to do that, so a stalemate occurs, with faith on one side and science on the other. The result is the wrong-headed impression that one cannot have faith if one has science, and that one cannot accept science if one has faith.

This is a very bad place for faith to be, because it makes faith look like fear. It makes the person of faith appear to the man of science as an ostrich who buries his head in the sand or as a child who plugs up her ears and hums a tune so she will not have to hear the disappointing truth and can go on pretending that her hopes for what she really wants are not in vain. This dichotomy, however, is also a bad place for people of science to be; for it forces them into a world without meaning or value—a world without hope and without love. From this point of view, life is what we make of it, but it does not go on beyond the material realities of our daily experience. This is all there is, nothing more. Nothing is finally inviolable. Nothing can lay claim to an absolute value, for all values are the values of contingent things. Everything we work to achieve, aspire to become, and cherish, must pass away into oblivion—even if only after billions of years—where no residual value endures.

There is, however, a middle way—a way that places before us the fundamental option that lies at the heart of the Bible and stands for us as its real "hermeneutical key": the key to understanding the Bible as the word of God. That fundamental option is the choice between a world founded on love and any other alternative. It is the choice between a world in which life triumphs over death and one in which death is the final arbiter of life. It is the fundamental option between hope and despair, and between communion and alienation. At the heart of this existential choice lies the difficulty of human suffering and how we are to make sense of it. Do we allow suffering to present itself in all its horrific self-evidence as the real conceptual challenge to our view of the universe? Or do we avoid the "challenge" of suffering and deal with it another way? In short, are we prepared to accept the challenge of the "problem of evil"? Or else, do we opt, instead, for a world in which *goodness* is the problem— the insoluble conundrum in the face of which we believe what we do about the world and its origins?

The Bible represents the *witness* of faith for all time, and presents for us, through myriad stories and images, discourses and canticles, prayers and proverbs, and even through more or less historical accounts, the fundamental option for a world founded on love. The ancient Jews saw themselves as uniquely free in the world for having perceived this truth, and they saw everyone who did not enjoy that freedom as a prisoner of darkness and ignorance, condemned to a life characterized by fear, in which there is no real reason to think that good could ever last in the end. These people, who did not know the truth about the way things really are—who did not know God—were called "gentiles", not because the Jews could not distinguish one culture from another, but because no further distinction mattered to them. There was a choice to be made between two worlds—one of life and the other of death. On the side of life stood the Jews, and on the side of death stood everybody else.[1]

This is the hermeneutical key to reading the Bible on its own terms, and for recovering what is truly at stake in the first creation narrative of the Old Testament. The point, as we will see, is to read the text not as offering a specific account of the exact manner in which God set out to bring the world into its present shape and form, but, instead, as setting before the reader the fundamental option between life and death, faith and faithlessness. This is what the first creation narrative of the Book of Genesis sets before us, and it is the focus of this book. It is hoped that, after walking with the reader through this text, we might see together in clearer light what being a person of faith really means, why that faith is worth sharing with others, and why it must never be given up to the "wisdom of this age."[2] It is hoped, also, that those who find themselves compelled by scientific discovery will find in our treatment here the enduring intelligibility of faith in God, and realize that entering into covenant with God does not require them to deny the facts of their experience, but, instead, that it means only accepting God's loving invitation to interpret the meaning of those facts through the prism of his sacred heart.

---

[1] Taken from the Roman usage, where it had referred to a purely secular, political distinction, the term "gentile" (*gentilis*) was adopted into the Judeo-Christian tradition with an entirely new point of reference. In Roman usage, the term represented the distinction between the Roman Empire and the non-Roman world, where the Roman form of political organization was seen as privileged above its alternatives—those of the "gentiles". Once appropriated into the Judeo-Christian tradition, however, the term's meaning was turned on its head in a powerfully symbolic way. On the covenantal criterion of God's self-revelation, where Israel stands as the paradigm, Rome itself is a "gentile" nation.

[2] 1 Corinthians 2:6.

CHAPTER 1

⁌

Babylonians in the Background

Today, scholars widely recognize that the pagan cultures surrounding ancient Israel bore an enormous influence on the composition of the Bible. It is not that we can look to the Bible and find explicit quotations from the pagan literature, but, instead, that, in the Bible, the people of God are engaged in a continuous critique of alternative worldviews. Throughout the Bible, they confront their pagan interlocutors as if to say, "Your view of the universe leads only to death and misery," or "Your take on this problem of human experience is incorrect and harmful to human happiness." To do this, they often borrow from familiar images and myths, recasting them in a distinctly

Hebrew light. Foremost among these pagan interlocutors are the Babylonians who held the Hebrew people in captivity for a period of roughly forty-eight years following their siege of Jerusalem. This "exile" gave rise, directly and indirectly to a great deal of the Old Testament, and became a fundamental dimension of the perennial Hebrew self-understanding. It ranks along-side the Exodus experience as one of the great formative events of the People Israel.

So, it should come as no surprise that, when we turn to the first chapter of the book of Genesis, we find the faint outlines of an ancient Babylonian myth, known to us today as the *Enûma Elish*. The first creation account (Genesis 1:1–2:4) is not a copy of that myth, but, instead, a confrontation of it. It belongs to the so-called "priestly voice" of the Old Testament, and reflects the ceremonial and liturgical consciousness of the People Israel. The priestly voice is not the oldest voice that speaks to us from the pages of the Old Testament, even though it is the first voice we encounter when we open the Bible. It comes to maturity at the time immediately following the exile in Babylon, when the Jewish people were given leave to return to their own land, to rebuild their Temple in Jerusalem, and to worship there once more.

After the Exile

It may well be the case that the Babylonians permitted the Jews to return to Jerusalem only because their exile had kept them two full generations and more away from their ritual homeland. In Catholic terminology, this span of time (forty or more years) is referred to as "time immemorial." It means that generational memory has been lost—that two generations have come to maturity and a third is on its way without a memory of what life had been like before. In the time of the Exodus, for example, the Jewish people had wandered through the desert in search of holiness and the Promised Land for a period of forty years, and God had sworn that, because of their persistent infidelity, most of the people who had left Egypt with Moses would not live to see their new home. The people who finally claimed the Promised Land had little memory of their bondage in Egypt, except as received through the stories of their parents' liberation.

If we imagine a pagan society vying with its neighbors for cultural dominance, then, we can understand why sacking a Temple—the locus of their worship and the very center of their cultural consciousness—would be an effective way to consign them to history, or, more precisely, to erase them from it. An extended period of exile would make the outcome nearly certain, since it would prevent the conquered nation from even beginning to rebuild for as long as they remained in captivity. It is easy to understand, from this perspective, why the Hebrew people saw their Babylonian neighbors as a complete antithesis of themselves. We can get a sense of the grief and anxiety felt by the Hebrew people, as well as the seething bitterness they felt toward their captors, when we read the Psalmist's lament, as he writes:

> By the rivers of Babylon, there we sat and wept as we remembered Zion. On the *arabim*, there, within their branches, we hung up our lyres. For there our captors asked us to sing songs; our tormentors [asked for] gladness, saying, "Sing a song

of Zion!" [But] how could we sing Yahweh's song in a foreign land?³

One can easily imagine that the scenario described in this Psalm is based in a concrete historical event—in an actual particular instance in which a group of exiles were remembering their homeland in conversation with some Babylonian natives, and what may have been a friendly request to share their own songs struck a raw nerve, reminding these exiles that they were captives, who were being driven to extinction by the people around them. Indeed, by the time the Jewish people returned from their Babylonian exile, it would have seemed unlikely that they could ever reemerge as a cultural force. The fight was over, it would have appeared. Their eventual assimilation into the Babylonian cult would have been little more than a matter of time.

To the surprise of their neighbors, however, history has a different story to tell. The Babylonians are gone from our sight, while the Jews remain. Once among the greatest and most powerful cultures on earth, they have gone so profoundly extinct that, until archaeologists recovered them from the rubble of history in the nineteenth century, the narratives of their mythology that had most profoundly influenced the Bible had been utterly lost to us. We had forgotten almost entirely *The Epic of Gilgamesh*, but the story of Noah and the Ark will be remembered forever. The *Enûma Elish* was unknown to the modern world, but the first creation narrative in Genesis is with us still. The Babylonians have vanished, but the Jewish people survived against all odds. God "remembered the promise he made to

---

[3] Psalm 137:1–4.

Abraham and his descendents,"[4] and preserved in his people a memory of the meaning of his Name.

So, when the Jews returned from their exile, their first priority was to "rebuild the walls of Jerusalem,"[5] and to restore an order of worship to the Elohistic Covenant. But a people so long dispersed throughout a foreign land had, by then, lost a sense of their own, unified narrative of history— they had lost the commonality of the stories they told to understand their place in the world. With their narrative continuity broken, how could it be restored?

The answer to this question is suggested to us in the book of Nehemiah, where we read that, upon the return of the people to Jerusalem and the restoration of the Temple, the priests and scribes led the people in an elaborate religious ceremony, at the heart of which stood the reading of the Torah. This reading spanned from early morning until midday, at the end of which the people wept as one, but rejoiced in their understanding of what they had heard.[6]

Many scholars believe that this passage recounts the formation of the Pentateuch or *the first five books of the Old Testament*. It is suggested that the priests and scribes had collected together the wide body of literature that had developed or survived during the time of the exile, and wove them together into a coherent common narrative that expressed the heart of the faith that still bound them together as one, in spite of everything. This is a plausible thesis. It would provide at least a hint as to how it came to be that obviously disparate textual elements now find themselves woven together as a whole, and how it follows from that

---

[4] Cf. Luke 1:54–55. Cf., also, Exodus 2:24, 32:13; Psalm 105:42.

[5] Psalm 51:18b.

[6] Nehemiah 8:1–12.

final product that the Jewish people, in spite of a thousand obstacles, were able to recover from their experience in Babylon a collective cultural memory of who they were in relationship to God.

Having said this, we need to understand what the substance of the choice is that lies at the heart of the Bible, and at the heart of the first creation narrative in the book of Genesis. We have already commented on this matter briefly, saying that the Bible presents for us a fundamental option between life and death, between communion and alienation, between a world founded on love and some alternative reality. All of that is true. But why is it so? What is it about the Judeo-Christian point of view that makes it so profoundly different from every other point of view? And why are all the alternatives, myriad though they are, treated by the ancient Jews as if they were really all the same—as if nothing else mattered about the views espoused by other peoples, but that they were different from those of the Jews?

Paganism and the Cosmos

To answer these questions, we have to bracket everything we already understand about God on the basis of revelation. We will have to pretend that the Judeo-Christian tradition does not exist for us. From this point of view, we must ask the primordial questions of human existence anew, as if we have no answers already in mind. "Why is there something rather than nothing? Have things always been as they are today? Why are things the way they are? What is the meaning of life? Why is there suffering and death for human beings who aspire to an inexhaustible future? Why is there evil in the world?"

These are not easy questions to answer. In fact, they represent the deepest mysteries of the common human experience. They lie at the foundation of all philosophy and all religion, and, thus, of every culture ever to emerge in the whole history of the human race. We are all well aware of the fact that our lives are not entirely our own—that we are subject to influences and forces beyond our control. Our lives do not turn out exactly as we wish, and, in the end, can go horribly wrong, even if we do everything right. There is some reality that transcends the horizon of our own limited mode of existence, and we depend upon it at every moment of our lives; but, in the final analysis, we have no direct experience of it, we do not really know what it is, and we have no real idea where we stand with it.

Allowing ourselves, in this way, to face the human condition in its most primal form, we immediately understand that, without the aid of revelation from God, we will have to attempt to answer our questions in the groping darkness of our own, limited, human point of view, based as it is upon only our foundational experiences. We will note that the experience of evil is rooted in the experience of suffering and death. We migrate from a state of health to a state of illness, and from a state of vigor to a state of death. Our primordial experience of evil, in other words, is the experience of the specter of death. This specter appears to us as a distinct "power" in the world—even as a power *over* the world, as it constrains within its inescapable reach everything we encounter in our daily lives. Every plant, every animal, and every human being comes into being and passes away. "Indeed," Paul reminds us, from top to bottom, "the structure of this cosmos passes-away."[7]

This primordial encounter with evil affords a rather dark starting point upon which to found a cultural perspective. But, on the other hand, every culture on earth represents some collective attempt at offering a response to the questions we have posed here, so we see already that human beings are almost "logically" prone to embrace a dark and terrifying outlook on the world. From the experience of evil as death, and death as a power, we see that the world suffers under the reign of death—the reign of evil—because it is susceptible to change. Youth, for example, gives way to old-age. Health can change into sickness, happiness into sorrow, love into hatred, and life into death. The ability to change makes evil possible.

Once this conclusion is drawn, our attempts to answer the primordial problems of human existence will take on a definite structure, no matter what particular theses we

---

[7] 1 Corinthians 7:31b. This passage does not lend itself to any easy English translation, but its sense is captured well by the standard approaches to translation, whereby it is rendered somewhat like, "For the present form of this world is passing away" (NRSV), or "For the world in its present form is passing away" (NAB), or "For the world as we know it is passing away" (REB). The Greek includes the word *scheima* (σχῆμα), which means, roughly, "an outline" or a "transitional or provisional structure." Thus, in his use of this term, Paul already means to say that for as long as the cosmos remains as it has been received by us, it will always be provisional—always passing away. This characteristic of the world—that the world as we know it is transitory and fleeting—is the world's true constant. Here, Paul has grasped the core of Heraclitus' philosophical despair, as he ended his career sitting by the banks of a stream wiggling his finger, replying to those who questioned him, "we cannot step into the same river twice, for all is flux." For a similar New Testament assessment of the cosmic predicament as that expressed here by Paul, see 1 John 2:17.

develop much further down the road, for we will have already staked out the horizon of our world within a certain frame. Having observed that evil in our world requires the ability to change, we begin to look within the structure of our world for all the roots of this ability. What changes? How do these things change? Is there anything that does not change? Is there any escape from change for the things that do?

Immediately, we will have to note that change occurs as a fundamental property of the material world, as St. Paul acknowledges in the passage we quoted above. Material beings come into existence and pass away. We are born, we grow, we deteriorate, and we die. The world of our experience goes around and around this way, seemingly forever.

This observation led the ancient pagan religions to adopt a basically cyclical understanding of time. There was no definite "progress" for the world, but, instead, an unending series of repetitions, in which the individual human life was like a microcosm of the universe itself: constantly coming to birth and passing away again. The ancient mythologies are rife with this sort of cosmology—a cosmology foreign, we must insist, to that of the Judeo-Christian tradition, according to which the world really is "going somewhere," with a promise that, in the end, it will all amount to something yet unimaginable in its glory. Paul reminds us of this fact when he declares that, "eye has not seen, ear has not heard, nor has [it] risen-up into the human heart what God has prepared for those who belong to him in love."[8]

But the pagan option has another characteristic much darker than the first. It is *dualistic*. The pagan mind sees the

---

[8] 1 Corinthians 2:9.

world as divided between a principle that accounts for life and a principle that accounts for death, a principle that accounts for goodness and a principle that accounts for evil. Evil, in other words, is viewed, again, as a "power"—as a positive principle in its own right, capable of acting on the world.

Once this move is made, we generally opt for a polytheistic worldview. If reality emerges from more than one principle, then there will also be more than one god in the universe. Some gods may rank higher than others, but because gods are associated with the shaping of the universe, multiple principles of being will require a pantheon in the heavens to give them form.

Typically, these gods are tied in some way to the forces and presences of our environment. There may be a god of the sun, a god of the moon, and a god of the ocean. We may even have gods who control our social environment, like a god of love or a god of war. But it will also be the case, generally speaking, that the pantheon will be divided between male and female gods—between gods and goddesses. The Judeo-Christian worldview looks nothing like this, and the implications of that difference will be profound, indeed.

Meanwhile, from the dualistic foundation that lies at the heart of the pagan worldview, we will begin to see a whole range of dichotomies emerging in our consciousness as we play through all the implications of the change/evil relationship. That which changes is evil. Thus, the physical world, the world of *ta physika* (τα φυσικά = that, in reality, which is subject to change) is evil. Within this broad horizon, whatever is directly linked to the physical, material dimension of reality will also be evil. At first, we see dichotomies like the following:

Good	Evil
Changeless	Changeable
Spiritual	Physical
Form	Matter
Mind	Body
Invisible	Visible
Order	Chaos
Light	Darkness

From here, we make other observations. We will note that reason grasps seemingly unchangeable realities. However it may be that this is so—and that is a philosophical conundrum all to itself—the fact is that we can retain the universal and timeless knowledge that, for example, $1+1=2$, long after the particular material objects that first brought that truth to our attention have passed from this world. We can add one piece of fruit to another and discover this relationship between them. We can build a line of men by adding the company of one to one. The fruit may be eaten and the men may die, but we still have access to the truth we learned that day—one of anything added to one of the same thing, equals two of that thing: $1+1=2$. This fact never changes. It is not subject to corruption, but endures beyond all time and space. Our awareness of it is, for us, an immaterial operation of some kind—an incorruptible act. Reason, therefore, does not come from evil. It comes from goodness. Reason is good. But what, then, will we have to say of emotion?

Emotion certainly belongs to the realm of change. Emotions or passions arise in us, assume varying degrees of intensity, abide for a time, and then fade away. Our emotions give way to one another, as happiness dissipates in sorrow, and fear transmutes into anger. Emotions change, so emotions are evil.

Paganism and the Feminine

At this point, we are approaching that quality of paganism that might seem most surprising to the modern observer, but also most disturbing. If the material world is generally evil, inasmuch as evil is directly linked to corruptibility, and emotions are seen, also, to belong to this sphere, then that in human beings which is most emotional and most bodily will consequently be the more evil in us as well.

Anyone familiar with the history of ancient philosophy from the time of the Pre-Socratics through the time of the Stoa will immediately recognize in this analysis the basic structure of thought reflected in the early history of Greek philosophy. Matter changes, and, with that, we contrast an unchanging dimension of spirit. Emotions change from one moment to another, and against this fleeting affection stands enduring reason. Against body stands mind. And, often, against feminine stands masculine, for the feminine form is perceived as more bodily than the masculine, more emotional, and even more primordial, characterized by a striking beauty that blossoms like a flower and then gradually fades away in the midst of a life of constant flux.

Without entering upon polemics, therefore, we should observe that, among human beings, sexual differentiation emerges, in the face of the pagan analysis, as a distinct problem. Women, as we have said, are seen as more bodily than men—as more material. Even the best of the pagan philosophers, who had thrown off the shackles of their cultural mythologies, still tended to think of women as under-developed human beings. Their reasoning on this point made sense, given what was available for them to know, but the scope of their knowledge was constricted to some extent by the narrow horizons of their pagan imagination. They thought that the higher pitch of the feminine voice was a mere hold-over from a childhood never fully outgrown, and that there was, in a similar way, a certain formlessness of a woman's uterine blood—the blood within her "void" as it was called—was, therefore, able to receive the imprint of the form of the man. For this reason, also, it was believed that a perfectly-formed offspring would simply be a perfect replication of the father. For Aristotle, women were very truly inferior to men—and that was a typically pagan point of view.

In fact, women do undergo day-to-day change more acutely than men do. From one week to another in the course of a month, a woman's bodily constitution is in constant and rather dramatic flux. Today, we understand the hormonal mechanisms, but this fact is not relevant here. We are interested in the primordial human assessment, and on that score, the people of the ancient world could observe the basic facts at least as well we can observe them today. Women were more bodily than men, they concluded. Women prefer to remain in one place, and they are more preoccupied than are men with their own physical condition, because they have to be. The woman herself is the medium through which bodily generation occurs, the baby growing within the space provided by the mother's own body, and being built up, seemingly, out of her very own flesh. Even newborns still take their food from the mother's own body, and we observe, even in the modern world, that a pregnant or nursing mother must take in extra nutrients because, as we say, "she is eating for two."

It is also generally observed that women are more emotional than men are. It is more accurate, perhaps, to say that women prioritize the authority of emotion in their experience of humanity, while men prioritize the authority of reason. While, of course, we will always be able to point to anecdotal exceptions to the general rule, we can say that male friends converse shoulder-to-shoulder, while female friends converse face-to-face. Of course, this is an exaggerated image, but it is not, for that reason, a misleading one. Any casual observer can see that men in conversation will tend to look off into the distance—into the world of abstraction—while women in conversation will lower their gazes to look into one another's eyes, intently. They will lean toward one another, especially if seated together, while men will tend to lean backward, heads tilted to the distant horizon, or to the stars.

This difference in bodily posture represents a difference in the approach taken to interpersonal relationships on the part of men and women. For men, relationships are forged and negotiated around rational boundaries—around shared concepts—while for women, relationships are forged and negotiated around emotional experiences. We generalize, of course, but only to make a point about the primordial assessment of the human condition, not to offer a critical treatment of gender psychology, which, in any event, would require a book of its own.

Unfortunately, if emotions are regarded as evil because they are subject to change, then the priorities of the feminine psyche mean that women cannot be trusted to make responsible judgments. They are unreliable at best and evil at worst, insofar as they are women, think like women, and respond like women. In fact, the threat against the feminine posed by the tendency of human culture to adopt false dichotomies takes us to even darker conclusions than those we have already considered. Not only are women evil in themselves and not to be vested with a public trust, they are carriers of evil—their evil is contagious.

In many pagan cultures, it is believed that the spiritual element in human beings belongs to an opposing order, or an opposing plane, from matter—in other words, that human beings are two separate realities, one spiritual and the other material, which do not really belong together. This view is typical, for example, among the Gnostic sects that were distributed in so many forms throughout Mesopotamia and the Nile River basin from about the second century before, through about the fourth century following, the advent of Jesus Christ. According to this general view, the soul belongs to the realm of spirit, yet finds itself imprisoned by the body, unable to escape its gravitational pull. This imprisonment of the body infects the soul's consciousness with concerns of a base and transient nature, imposing an amnesia of all the truths to which the soul, as an element of unchanging spirit, already holds, but can no longer access in the fog of fleeting passions, hungers, and bodily drives.

Sex involves these powerful bodily drives and intense passions. And it also supplies the mechanism, on this worldview, for the imprisonment of souls in matter. It begins when a man finds himself drawn to a woman, whom he then pursues with ever-growing intensity. As he seeks her, he becomes more like the object of his desire, prioritizing emotion over reason, and adopting a face-to-face posture at the expense of a shoulder-to-shoulder companionship oriented to a world of ideas. Abandoning that world for the object of his desire, he enters, instead, a world of feelings and bodies. When he does, other souls will be forced to pay the price for his indiscretion: children will be born—spirits imprisoned in bodies for the crimes of their father, who, for his own part, had succumbed to the contagion of feminine evil.

We are not interested, of course, in defending this assessment, since, in fact, it has nothing at all in common with the biblical worldview.[9] Our purpose, here, is only to describe and explain. The ancient Hebrew people were responding to what they saw as a grossly distorted view of reality, and we will not understand the significance of their reply unless we understand the basic contours of the worldview against which it was directed.

So, once again, in an attempt to understand the primordial assessment of the human condition, we should consider the fact that when men approach women romantically, they begin to take on feminine traits in that relationship. The converse is not the case. Women do not express romantic interest in men by standing with them shoulder-to-shoulder and looking out to the distant horizon of ideas. Indeed, men would not even recognize that posture as indicative of romantic interest. Rather, women continue to behave like women and draw men to adopt those behaviors for themselves. As a man begins to discover romantic interest, he expresses it in a bodily turn toward his beloved. He leans toward her, softens his voice, lowers his brow, and gazes into her eyes. If the woman, or at least, femininity, is regarded as evil—if that is our starting point—then this transformation of masculine behavior according to a feminine profile would be regarded as pitiable. It would

---

[9] It is helpful to note, on this point, that women in ancient Hebrew culture were expected to be every bit as literate as men, while laws against female literacy were common in pagan societies, and remain so today.

represent a sad and humiliating failure, regardless of the fact that it happens in the life of nearly every man on earth.

From this point of view, the feminine appears as the very symbol of the evil of the material world. It must be constrained and controlled lest, allowed to run free, the world would be consumed entirely by the chaos of flux, emotion, and our bodily drives. Women are seen as noble, then, only insofar as they can assume a posture of asexuality—a posture in which they can be seen as having risen above their bodiliness to become spiritual.

From this vantage point, three features of the pagan world come clearly into view. First, virginity is to be valued as a uniquely feminine virtue—a virtue for women, in particular, because it represents an asexual mode of existence for them. In virginity, a woman remains aloof from the implications of her radical materiality, and frees men from the power of her seduction. Because this is the case, the assumption of a sexual posture on the part of a woman, even in the context of marriage, is seen to diminish her. She is sullied in the sexual act, even in marriage, such that her value is reduced by marriage to the level of mere utility.

In extreme cases, this revaluation of the woman through sex can lead us to see women as worthless to society upon the death of their husbands. The practice of *sati* (सती), in which a woman is immolated atop her deceased husband's funeral pyre is reflective of this attitude. If she remained in this world, she could beg for food or serve as a prostitute if anyone would still desire her. But if she could transcend her bodiliness with her deceased husband, and only then, she would become an object of veneration.

The second feature we wish to point out, however, is that because the noblest value of a woman is destroyed in marriage, polygamy comes to be seen as a natural value.

Women are commodities that lose most of their value on their wedding night. With the bodily stresses of repeated pregnancy and age, what remains of their worth diminishes further over time, until a man simply desires what we would call today, an "upgrade." As is generally the case in the acquisition of commodities, the well-to-do are more likely to be able to take advantage of them, and the wealthy and powerful surround themselves with harems while the average man must content himself with one wife, or no wife at all. This latter eventuality is not seen, culturally, as a mere curse, because, hidden beneath it lies the freedom of the celibate man from the moral vortex of the feminine.

This fact helps us to understand how the third feature of the treatment of women in pagan society could be sustained through the generations. If women are seen as inherently ignoble or even evil—if the world really needs fewer women and more men—then the tendency will be to value sons over daughters. There is no question that this trait is common among pagan cultures, generally speaking. In the least offensive cases, we see the societies in which daughters represent a burden to their families. To escape this burden, a fee is paid to another family if a daughter should be taken in matrimony. In the worst cases, however (and these cases are prevalent both in ancient times and in our own), daughters are simply abandoned to the elements or actively killed. Today, the ability to determine the sex of the offspring during pregnancy leads, undeniably, to sex-selective abortions, such that, in some societies, we find simply unsustainable ratios of male to female births. We find this problem both in India and China, for example. In the ancient world, however, people had to wait until birth and deal with the problem then. Infanticide, whether direct or indirect (i.e. in the form of exposure to the elements), was rampant.

Indeed, the obvious preference of the masculine over the feminine is reflected in archaeological finds in which masses of babies, presumably females, have been recovered from graves and drainage ditches at ancient Mesopotamian sites. It is also reflected in the fact that human sacrifice in the ancient world more often than not involved female victims. It is likely that these poorly-understood practices reflected the kind of sensibility to which we referred earlier, namely, that the transcendence of the bodily form of her existence was a woman's noblest act. Leaving the world of the body would have meant rejecting the evil within, cleansing the world of the element of her own nefarious influence, and, thus, atoning for sin.

In our own time, it is difficult for us to appreciate the relationship between the pagan world and the oppression of women. We are given to imagining that Christianity is responsible for this offense, mainly on the grounds that women cannot receive ordination in the Catholic Church— nor, for that matter, in any of the Orthodox churches. This is not the place to address that accusation directly. What concerns us here is the presentation of a broadly pagan perspective on women—a perspective grounded in the overarching presuppositions at the foundation of a pagan view of the universe. Again, we are well aware of the fact that we can speak here only in generalities; we cannot begin to address all the variants of pagan cultures throughout the world and across time. A project of that nature would require an encyclopedia, and would likely never reach completion. That is not the task we have set before ourselves. For our purposes, we need only sketch out the broad contours of a generally pagan worldview as it relates to the oppression of women, and point out that, in actual historical fact, this relationship does exist, at least as a general characteristic of paganism considered as a whole, even if, today, many women experience themselves as free, even in societies that do not have Judeo-Christian roots.

This fact can be explained by the strong, normativizing influence of western culture across much of the globe. In fact, however, beyond the scope of that influence, women throughout the world live under a veil of oppression—in some instances, quite literally—even today. The tendency to blame Christianity for this oppression should be countered by sober reflection upon the cultures in which this sort of oppression actually does take place, and in what forms. No argument is even necessary here once we recognize that the woman currently reading this book almost certainly lives either in a historically Judeo-Christian society, or else in a society that has been heavily influenced by the West, which itself is historically Judeo-Christian. We would not be having this conversation at all in a genuinely pagan culture.

But how could such widespread marginalization of women ever happen in the first place? How could cultures like these ever emerge at all, much less most of the time? And how could they survive for hundreds and even thousands of years on that foundation? Indeed, it is almost impossible to believe that such widespread oppression takes place solely at the bidding of men. Keeping half the population in bondage—indeed, the half with the most direct influence upon the emerging generation—requires their complicity. If we remember that we are speaking here of a primordial assessment of the human condition, it is not at all difficult to see how this could happen. Once we accept the false dichotomies characteristic of a pagan view of the universe, the marginalization of the feminine follows as a matter of course. It will be accepted as a basic truth that explains why the world looks as it does. What matters, we must understand, is not that the account we give of the human condition is a comforting one, but that it helps us to make sense out of our experience, even if the sense it helps us make is the sense of doom and despair. We know from our own experience that, in the face of an incomprehensible sorrow—for example, the fact of death, which everyone must face at some point—any explanation is better than no explanation. When the horrors of human suffering press in upon us, we instinctively seek a way out of the meaning-void that exists in the absence of an explanation. We ask, "Why did this happen?" The existentialist philosophers of the nineteenth and twentieth centuries knew as well as the people of the ancient world that any explanation, no matter how dark and terrifying, is better than no explanation at all.[10]

---

[10] We should note, however, that this knowledge did not prevent the existentialist philosophers from opting, in some instances, against any explanation at all. The advent of *nihilism* among the existentialists (and this is not to suggest that existentialism is always nihilistic) arises when no explanation for the structure of reality can meet the evidential requirements of our philosophical presuppositions. In other words, in any set of philosophical presuppositions, we bracket evidence, either allowing it or disallowing it into a system of explanations, depending upon whether it conforms to our foundational presuppositions or not. Philosophical reasoning involves a process of "filtering" what at first "appears" as reality, and testing it against carefully defined criteria. A great deal of argument has taken place in the history of philosophy over establishing those criteria, precisely because everything else we do from that point forward depends upon whether we have gotten our criteria right or not. In the case of the nihilists, they have defined their criteria to exclude anything of the sort that would allow for the interpretation of meaning in the universe, and have, thus, precluded the possibility of escaping the "meaning-void" to which we referred above. This is what Jean Paul Sartre means by the phrase, "No Exit" in his 1944 play by that title, in which three damned souls must resign themselves to the absurdity that characterizes their state. He is offering a metaphor for the actual state of our present life, which he sees as

For this reason, the characteristically dark and terrifying worldviews typically adopted by pagan cultures are found acceptable, simply because they do represent accounts of the basic problems of the human condition. They appeal on that basis alone. They come, however, at a terrible cost—a cost borne mostly by women. In the pagan world, because the feminine is seen as generally defective or evil, violence must be done to them in one way or another; and, when it is, it is seen to be a good, not only for men, but for women as well, and for the world.

Paganism has been attempting to reassert itself in western society for at least the past hundred and fifty years, with the rise of materialist explanations of reality, like that advanced by Karl Marx. We use the term "paganism" here in precisely the same way that the ancient Hebrew people used the word "gentile". It does not necessarily indicate any specifically religious perspective, even if, as a matter of historical fact, everyone was, in some sense, religious in the Mesopotamian world at the time the Torah was first being written. "Paganism" indicates, for our purposes here, only the alternative, whatever it is, to the Judeo-Christian worldview. In our own world, this usually means a decidedly scientistic, materialistic, atheistic worldview. In some ways, perhaps, this new paganism, however "enlightened" it sees itself to be, may be even darker and more terrifying than the ancient varieties, for it is a world devoid of any explanation.

With the influence of this "neo-paganism" upon western culture, we can see, once again, rather clearly if we are paying attention, the fact that a general hostility to the feminine has returned. The distinctive quality of femininity as fertility and generativity is seen as a threat to the

---

inherently absurd—that is to say, without any explanation but that which we would impose upon the world by our own will.

equilibrium of society and the health of the world. Humanity is the problem, and the feminine propensity to pregnancy and childbirth simply exacerbates it. It comes to be seen, then, as good for women to sterilize them, making them more like men, and thus, ennobling them.

Today in the United States, for example, the Catholic Church finds itself embroiled in a battle for religious freedom against a government regime dominated by a contemporary neo-pagan, secularist philosophy. The federal government is attempting to conscript all Americans, including those with principled moral objections, into funding hormonal contraceptives and sterilization procedures for any woman in the nation who desires them. This initiative represents exactly the characteristically pagan hostility to women we have been attempting to elucidate in these pages. In spite of the fact that these interventions undeniably mean impairing the normal organismic functioning or bodily integrity of a perfectly healthy woman—artificially producing a disease state in the woman, or else mutilating her, treating her fertility as a medical "problem"—and in the face of overwhelming evidence that the use of hormonal contraceptives also greatly increases serious health risks for women in the long run, the initiative is proposed to society as a moral good more important for the health of society than religious liberty or the right to conscientious objection. To restore balance to the ecosystem and the economy, the noblest thing for a woman to do in this neo-pagan world, is, once again, to transcend her bodiliness—the fact of her feminine distinction.

We mention this issue, not to politicize the Bible, which, after all, remains the focus of the present work, but to point out that the central question posed by the Bible remains a question for us today. If, at the heart of the Bible, we face a fundamental option for a world founded on love or some other world instead, this option is as real for us today as it was when the oldest stories in the Bible were first being told in their original historical and cultural context. The Bible is not just a book for the past, but a book for the present and future as well. It is *our* book—a book in which God speaks to us today, and carries on with us the very same conversation he first started with Abraham that starry night so long ago, when he called him out of paganism.[11]

The Babylonian Alternative?

The Babylonian myth of origins is known today as the *Enûma Elish*. It is a truly ancient tale.[12] Most scholars believe that it dates to around the seventeenth or sixteenth century BC. It survives not on papyrus but on stone tablets, and is written in a primitive alphabet known as cuneiform in an extinct Semitic language called Akkadian. The *Enûma Elish* is a lengthy narrative, featuring redundancies and overlapping typologies. It is, in other words, character-

---

[11] The name, Abraham (אַבְרָהָם), both in this covenantal form and in its original form (Abram = אַבְרָם), means, "exalted father." It indicates that he will be the great patriarch of all the heirs of the promise of love and providence he receives from God in faith as a definitive act of God's self-revelation. He was born in Ur of Chaldee (Genesis 11:27, 31; Nehemiah 9:7), in the regions of Babylon, and, thus, represents the triumph of the Yahwistic/Elohistic Covenant over the Babylonian cults as representatives of paganism in general.

[12] The name is taken from the first words of the poem. It means something like, "when on-high," "when the heavens," or "when the sky above." In this way, the beginning line of this myth ("When the heavens were not named") is similar to that of the first chapter of Genesis ("In the beginning, Elohim created the heavens and the earth" [Genesis 1:1]).

istically "primitive." It is also highly anthropomorphic, describing a realm of the gods capable of merging with earth because, like earth, the divine realm is essentially corporeal, at least in some sense. The world is formed out of originally "divine material" in the *Enûma Elish*. This idea is a fairly common feature of paganism in general, because, in paganism, the realm of the gods is typically seen as a dimension of the cosmos in some sense, and not as a mode of being totally transcendent of the world, as is the divine being in the Judeo-Christian worldview. Again, in ancient paganism, as in the New Age movement in our own time, "matter" and "spirit" belong to opposing planes of existence, but to the same order of reality. They are not perceived to exist in total otherness. Such an idea—that "spirit" belongs outside the cosmos altogether—simply has nothing to do with the Babylonian view of the universe.

Indeed, the *Enûma Elish* envisions a world precipitating out of evil, formed of the dismembered body of the evil dragon goddess Tiamat, who, as Mother of all gods, is the primordial substrate of all reality. The world, in spite of all that is good in it, remains evil at its core, on this model, and, as evil, must be constrained and controlled. Humanity, likewise, is formed out of the life-blood of Qingu, who plotted to disturb the order of the gods, leading to the cosmic conflagration that now necessitated the invention of humanity as a mitigating measure against perpetual anarchy. In some supremely pessimistic readings of this myth, humanity is formed of the blood of Tiamat.

At base, the differences between the *Enûma Elish* and the first creation narrative in Genesis can be reduced to a difference in their understanding of reality, of its meaning, and of its value, in light of the experience of the mystery of human existence. Once again, our foundational experience with evil as evil, we should recall, is death—the fact of death as it presents itself as an inescapable problem in all our lives. Death finalizes our sufferings, placing limits on our future hopes and aspirations. It imposes a claim to authority in moral matters, as failure to compromise our moral principles means facing the threat of death, or the threat of a life diminished in its prospects for happiness until, inevitably, death overtakes us, and that, too soon for us to change our plight for the better. This fact about our lives demands an explanation—*any* explanation—or else, what remains of life in the shadow of death becomes unbearable to us.

It is at this moment that the significance of the Babylonian response to this problem in the form of the myth of the *Enûma Elish* becomes clear as a contrast to the Hebrew response represented in the Bible. In the Babylonian myth, Tiamat, the dragon of chaos, we must recall, is a feminine figure, so the feminine among humans would represent a fuller manifestation of primordial evil than would the masculine. This degradation of the feminine is consistent with what we have already seen to be characteristic of the generally pagan, dualistic response to the primordial questions of human existence. But in the case of the Babylonian view, the specifics are especially grim. On the model articulated in the *Enûma Elish*, primordial evil is more powerful, in the end, than goodness, because the good god, Marduk—who is male—is, himself, the offspring of Tiamat. The only interpretation possible here is that the world is evil from top to bottom, and human women are the fullest form of evil in the material universe.

This outlook may explain why the role of the priestess in ancient Mesopotamian religion was not a prestigious role at all, by today's standards, but, instead, an occasion of abuse in the form of temple prostitution. In many ancient pagan cults, temple prostitution served as a ritual of passage, and every young woman in the society would be offered up in this way, sacrificially, at some point in her life, prior to marriage.[13] The abuse of the feminine can be seen, thus, to represent a rejection of the evil that lurks within. It represents a kind of "mortification of the flesh" for humanity as a whole, in our quest to appease the gods by joining them in their hostility to the primordial darkness out of which the world was formed.

The Hebrew view of the universe is totally different, and the first creation narrative in Genesis exists in part to make that exact point. Given, again, in the wake of their return from exile among the Babylonians, it is designed to restore to Israel a cultural memory of God's self-revelation and the fundamentally optimistic view of the universe that goes along with it. At the foundation of that worldview, and what accounts for its underlying optimism, is an absolutely new and unique idea in the ancient world known only to the People Israel: the idea of *creation*.

---

[13] See, for example, Sir James George Frazer, *The Golden Bough* (New York: The Macmillan Co., 1922), 330–331.

CHAPTER 2

∾

The Idea of Creation

The idea of creation, properly speaking, is not at all a philosophical concept, but a distinctly theological one. Neither is it a generally religious idea, but belongs, instead, entirely and uniquely to the Judeo-Christian tradition. The first creation narrative in the book of Genesis advances this unique concept as central to the worldview that distinguishes the People Israel from any other culture on earth. It consists in the idea that there exists a God who totally transcends the cosmos, and wills it into existence. It is the belief that there is one source of all reality, and it wills to bring into existence something other than itself. Before the Hebrew people embraced their Covenant with *Yahweh*

Elohim, no one had ever dared to think this way about the world.

We have already discussed how the dualistic worldview typical of the pagan response to the problems of human existence tended, generally, to lead to polytheism—to the belief that there are many gods to account for the various "powers" we experience in our world. In fact, the most primitive religions we know of are *animist* in character. Animism is the belief that the world is simply filled with "gods" or "spirits" from top to bottom. On this view, there are spirits particular to virtually every experience of our lives, to every time, every place, every object, and every sort of event to which we find ourselves exposed. Even the homes in which we live, and which we build with our own hands, might have their own distinctive spirits to which homage is expected to be paid lest some misfortune should arise.

While this view of the universe is decidedly "primitive," it is not, for that reason, simply to be rejected out of hand, even if it also happens to be false. The fact is that animistic religions reflect a basic truth about reality—namely, that nothing in our experience is beyond the reach of the spiritual. In Judeo-Christian terminology, we would say that "nothing escapes God's providence." We might note, then, a certain similarity between this primitive animistic sensibility and St. Thomas' provocative comment to the affect that, "God is in all things as their causal agent, who sustains them by his power."[14]

But, in the case of animism, there is no sense of a spiritual dimension of reality that utterly transcends the horizons of the world. The heavens are not wholly other, but,

---

[14] Cf. *Summa Theologiae* I.8.i.

in some sense, another dimension of the same reality shared by the material world. From this point of view—a view that remained a feature of paganism even in its more advanced forms—the realm of the gods is subject to limitations that, while different from those of time and space, are no less real for them. Gods, for example, are restricted in their activities by the limitations of their own power—by the boundaries of their province of influence, and, thus, by other gods who enjoy distinct powers of their own.

But, as animism is transcended by later polytheism, we find that the boundary between the material and the spiritual dimensions of reality appears to grow sharper, until, in the end, the gods no longer really wish to be involved directly in human life. This sensibility emerges as a reflection of the dualism characteristic of the pagan view of the universe, according to which that which is material is seen as somehow defective or even evil, and, in any event, beneath the dignity of the gods. These gods do not desire human company, and do not particularly like us. They tolerate our existence for reasons of their own, and employ us in their service to their own advantage, showing us favor only as it suits them, like a master might show kindness to a pet whom he would never permit to dine with him at table.

The evidence for this reading of paganism lies in the fact that pagan worship normally occurs outside the temple, typically at the top of a staircase. In some instances, for example, in the case of the ancient Parthenon devoted to the goddess Athena, the sacrificial staircase was located adjacent to the temple itself, which, for its own part, was designed with steps absurdly high so as to deter any human visitors from approaching the deity. For the pagans, the gods did not wish to be bothered by us, and the temple represented a sort of fortress. It was a no-man's land between heaven and earth, below which the gods did not wish to descend, and above which no human being could rise. In this context, sacrifice took on the character of appeasement and placation. It served to keep the gods at arm's length, and to stay their impatience with human annoyances, lest they strike us down in anger and disgust.

Sharp as the boundary is between heaven and earth on this polytheistic pagan model, the gods still remain, fundamentally, features of the cosmos itself, subject to at least some of the same laws that govern us mortals as well. They cannot simply do whatever they want; there are realities in the cosmic structure they are powerless to change, and attempts to reach beyond what belongs to them to do will cause them to face, just as we do, the inelasticity of the universe's proper form, as "fate" (*moira* [μοίρα] or *karma* [कर्म]) redounds upon their actions to restore "shape" to justice.

Gods of this sort cannot *create* in the proper sense. They do not properly impose being on nothingness, because they possess no direct power over being as such. At best, they act as "demiurges," who can shape the material potentialities of being, thereby structuring being in ways that suit their needs. When Marduk made human beings out of the blood of Qingu in the *Enûma Elish*, he was acting, not as a *creator*, but as a *demiurge*. This is a critically important conceptual distinction that is too frequently overlooked by contemporary scholars.

When the Greek philosophers finally abandoned polytheism in favor of monotheism—a move which unquestionably represented a colossal intellectual advancement—they remained, in spite of that insight, bound by the limitations of their fundamentally pagan way of thinking. Aristotle, for example, still thought of God as a feature of the cosmos, which, for its own part, was directly linked to him as a natural effect of his mode of existence. Aristotle's God was nothing like the God of the Bible, who thinks about human beings, and binds himself, not out of necessity but out of choice, to every particular being in the universe he wills into existence and holds in the palm of his hand. On the contrary, Aristotle's God is still completely pagan. Because he is the greatest thing there is, he finds himself unrivaled as an object of concern. For this reason, as "pure thought," he thinks only of himself; there simply is no better thing for him to think, so he finds himself, as it were, paradoxically limited by his own transcendence.

Aristotle's famous passage to this affect is given in his *De Anima*, where he describes the relationship between the provisional intellectual activity of human beings and the perfect intellectual activity of God. He explains that our changeable, contingent intellect is radically dependent upon the unchanging intellect of God, as pure thought. But his explanation also betrays his pagan prejudices; such a being would never—indeed, *could* never—deign to care for us. He writes:

> And in fact thought, as we have described it, is what it is by virtue of becoming all things, while there is another which is what it is by virtue of making all things: this is a sort of positive state like light; for in a sense light makes potential colours into actual colours.
>
> Thought in this sense of it is inseparable, impassible, unmixed, since it is in its essential nature activity (for always the active is superior to the passive factor, the originating force to the matter).
>
> Actual knowledge is identical with its object: in the individual potential knowledge is in time prior to actual knowledge, but absolutely it is not prior even in time. It does not sometimes think

and sometimes not think. When separated it is alone just what it is, and this alone is immortal and eternal . . . .[15]

Even if we could arrive at an absolutely transcendent God—a God utterly beyond nature—we would still, however, find ourselves unable to arrive at the idea of *creation*. The answer to the question of the existence of contingent being would remain an unanswerable conundrum. Why, if such a God does exist, would he ever create, knowing that his creature could not increase his own perfection, could not add to him in any way, and would, if anything, fall short of his own standard, if only by the fact of its contingency? Indeed, beyond the question of *why* such a God would create, there arises the additional difficulty already indicated in Aristotle's thesis—that he *could not do so* because he could never think of anything other than himself.

The idea of creation, as we have said, is utterly unique to the Judeo-Christian tradition, and it depends entirely upon the Hebrew understanding of God. We cannot emphasize strongly enough, however, that this understanding of God is not the product of any purely philosophical reflection, but comes, instead, from what the Judeo-Christian tradition refers to as "revelation." This term, we should be clear, is not strictly synonymous with the term "scripture." Rather, scripture gives a normative and perpetual textual expression to revelation, which, in the proper sense, should be

---

[15] Aristotle, *De Anima* III.5, 430^{a}14–24. We rely, here, upon the translation by J. A. Smith in Jonathan Barnes, ed., *The Complete Works of Aristotle: The Revised Oxford Translation*, Vol. 1, (Bollingen Series LXXI • 2. Princeton: Princeton University Press, 1984), 641–692. The erroneous phrasing, "this *above* is immortal" which appears in Smith's translation as printed in the Barnes edition is corrected in our rendering, "this *alone* is immortal" (430^{a}24).

understood as God's personal self-disclosure before creature. It is from within the context of this divine self-disclosure to humanity, that is to say, that the Hebrew conception of God is formed, and with it, the idea of creation.

In other words, the concept of creation comes from the experience of encounter with God—an encounter in which God discloses himself before us as he really is, and in a way that simply transcends all our human preconceptions about what is really possible at all. Through this encounter, to which the Bible repeatedly gives expression of the quality and content in the pivotal episodes of the history of salvation, God reveals himself as *Yahweh Elohim*. But what does it mean to say this? What does it mean to think of God in these terms? And how does it lead us to affirm the distinctly Judeo-Christian dogma of *creation*?

The name *Yahweh* is God's proper name, as revealed to Moses in the book of Exodus, when Moses experiences his theophany in the burning bush.[16] This story involves a profound paradox, in that, while the name Yahweh indicates God's radical transcendence and absolute freedom from all coercion and manipulation,[17] the possession of another's

---

[16] Exodus 3:1–19.

[17] A good, if brief, analysis of the implications of the name *Yahweh* (יְהֹוָה) can be found in Demetrius Dumm, O.S.B., *Flowers in the Desert: A Spirituality of the Bible* (New York, Paulist Press, 1987), 77–82. Father Demetrius notes, as a point of great relevance to our broader discussion, that the term is presented, in Hebrew, in the *imperfect tense*, which always connotes, in that linguistic tradition, an *unfinished action* (78). He goes on to note that the linguistic connotations of the Greek and Latin renderings are not as well-suited to communicate this nuance, but, instead, tend to obfuscate the dimensions of *event* and *encounter* by introducing the statically *theoretical*. Joseph Ratzinger makes a similar set of observations in his

name in the ancient Mesopotamian world was considered to represent an interpersonal advantage. Parents possess authority over their children, and express that fact in the act of naming them. That prerogative belongs to them because it both flows from and serves to ensure the parents' standing with respect to their children. In religious contexts, the magical rights associated with priests and wizards involved conjuring rituals, in which gods were invoked through the mystical utterance of their names. For God to reveal his name to Moses, and, through him, to the People Israel, means for him to assume a posture of vulnerability before them. He gives them the means to approach him, and to call upon him. In case we doubt these implications of the revelation of his name, we need only look to what God, himself says about the implications of his name in the story in question. He declares:

> You will say, therefore, to the sons of Israel, "Yahweh, the God your fathers—the God of Abraham, the God of Isaac, and the God of Jacob—has sent me to you." This is my name forever, and this is my memorial-name[18] to all generations. Go and gather the

---

Introduction to Christianity, J. R. Foster, trans. (San Francisco: Communio Books/Ignatius Press, 1969, 1990), 77–93. Another exceptional and thorough treatment of the meaning of the name Yahweh as understood through the lens of the Exodus narrative is provided by Martin Buber, in his book, *The Prophetic Faith*, Carlyle Witten-Davies, trans. (New York: Harper & Row, Publishers, 1960), 24–30.

[18] זִכְרִי = *zikrī*. This term is not easy to translate into English because we do not have any direct cognate to it. It indicates the act and content of our memory of another person, and, thus, possesses reverential and covenantal implications. God is saying, "This is how people will think of me throughout the generations. They will remember me as the God who binds himself to his people, who cares for them, and seeks to

elders of Israel and say to them, "Yahweh, the God of your fathers: the God if Abraham, Isaac, and Jacob, has revealed himself,[19] saying, 'I am deeply concerned about you, and what has been done to you in Egypt.[20]'"

In this narrative, God appears as the one who, while radically transcendent as the source of all being in the world,[21] nonetheless opens himself to the presence of his creature and makes himself approachable. This is the great mystery of the Judeo-Christian God, but the question of how it can be that he is like this calls for further reflection.

If we think of the term *Yahweh* as indicating the radical transcendence of God, while at the same time communicating by the fact of God's self-disclosure to his people the fact that he is intimate with us and approachable—a God who can be "deeply concerned" for his people, and who both remembers them and seeks to be remembered by them, then

---

bless them, not out of any obligation or manipulation, but out of his own absolute freedom and goodness."

[19] נִרְאָה אֵלַי = *nir'āh 'êlay*. This phrase is frequently translated, "has appeared to me," but it means, more precisely, "has rendered himself visible," or, "has shown-forth." The implication is that of *theophany* or *divine manifestation*, which, in this context, is associated with God's self-disclosure or self-revelation.

[20] Exodus 3:15–16. Even here, the relational orientation of Yahweh Elohim is clear, as he does not literally refer to "Egypt" as a place, but as a people whom he knows personally, and with whom he shares a history. Looking back to the story of the great flood with the righteous Noah and his three sons, God refers to the Egyptians as a people he had saved, long ago, in his mercy: בְּמִצְרָיִם = *bəmiṣrāyim* or "sons of Ham".

[21] אֶהְיֶה אֲשֶׁר אֶהְיֶה = *'eyeh 'ăšer 'eyeh* or "I am who I am." This self-attestation indicates both the fact of God's radical transcendence as Yahweh (יְהוָה) and the implications of that fact in terms of his total absolute freedom from constraint and coercion.

it is the term *Elohim* that opens the way to grasping the *how* of this terrifying mystery. The term *Elohim* (אֱלֹהִים) derives from the word *eloah* (אֱלוֹהַ), as its plural form. The word *eloah*, then, is a term that indicates great power and authority, whether on earth or in the heavens. It can be used adjectivally to describe, for example, the force of one's passion or one's resolve. It can be applied to a prince or a king, or to any person of great influence, or to an angel, a deity, or a demon. The term *Elohim*, therefore, is very certainly a paradox all by itself, for if anything distinguishes the Hebrew worldview from the worldview of any of their neighbors, it is the fact of their monotheism. Why, then, would their term for God—for their own God, and, in their view, the only true God—be rendered in a plural form?

Many scholars today, noting the historical relationship between the early Hebrews and their pagan neighbors, suggest that this plural form is merely a holdover from their polytheistic past—from before Abraham entered into Covenant with Yahweh. This thesis is simply incoherent, however, since the term is used throughout the Bible, even in those passages, like the first creation narrative in the book of Genesis, for example, which are composed with the clear purpose of distancing the Hebrew worldview from pagan polytheism. It would make no sense to retain an intrinsically polytheistic term at the very moment one is attempting to articulate precisely the opposite thesis about the realm of the divine. Yet, there is the word—*Elohim*—to describe the One True God. What does it mean?

God has disclosed himself to his people—an act that later pagan monotheistic philosophers would have thought impossible. As we explained above, for the pagan monotheists, an absolutely transcendent God would never be able to attend to any concern beneath its dignity or perfection. Their reasoning on this score is, in fact, a precursor to the reasoning of the theologians of the Middle Ages, who applied this logic to the human intellect, and said that the security of heaven rested in the fact that no alternative object could ever draw the mind and will away from the vision of God in the fullness of his glory, once it was apprehended in its own essence. Whatever we may say about the apprehension of the divine essence by a created beholder, however, this view has little, in fact, to do with the biblical portrait of God himself.

Indeed, the God of the Hebrew people is a God who attends to the needs and concerns of others as if they were his own. He is a God who thinks about others and cares about the affairs of his people in the world. He is a God who consciously and intentionally wills into being something other than himself, who *creates* and sustains all things, because—and this is the real key indicated by the term *Elohim*—his oneness is not a mere *monism*, but *relation*. The God of the Bible is spoken of as a plurality, and yet, "is one, while there is no other;"[22] he is at once radically transcendent and capable of thinking of someone else. This concept, expressed in the Bible by the joining-together of the God's proper name and descriptive designation—*Yahweh Elohim*—represents the root insight about the divine that distinguishes the Hebrew view of the universe from every conceivable alternative. It is the concept that allows for the idea of creation, and the revelation of it in God's self-

---

[22] We paraphrase here the words of the *Sh'ma* (the Jewish confessional prayer), the first words of which are taken from Deuteronomy 6:4, which reads, "*Sh'ma, Israel, Yahweh Eloheinu Yahweh Ehad*" (אֶחָד יְהוָה אֱלֹהֵינוּ יְהוָה יִשְׂרָאֵל שְׁמַע) or "Hear, Israel: Yahweh [is] our God, [and] Yahweh [is] One!" The word *Eloheinu* (אֱלֹהֵינוּ) derives from *Elohim* as its first person plural possessive form.

disclosure to his people makes creation a genuine *dogma* of the Faith.

St. John the Divine, in fact, comes to see the mystery of Jesus Christ through exactly this lens, and articulates the meaning of the paradoxical designation, *Yahweh Elohim* in his famous aphorism, "God is love."[23] Indeed, the content of the phrase *Yahweh Elohim* is expressed perfectly in this way. And it is precisely this affirmation—that God is love—that allows us, and, indeed, requires us to believe in creation. From within the Judeo-Christian tradition, which consists in the affirmation that the foundational reality is not merely some impersonal metaphysical principle, but *Love*, the world can no longer be thought of as a mere accident, unintended consequence, necessary evil, or side-effect. Rather, the Judeo-Christian world is a world loved into being by God, known to him and cherished by him. It is a world made for holiness, in which only goodness has the status of being, and evil is powerless before it, because, in itself, it is nothing at all.

---

[23] 1 John 4:16.

CHAPTER 3

୰

The Structure and Purpose of the Genesis Narrative

We have already discussed the background of the narrative of the seven days of creation—the "Genesis narrative"—providing a brief treatment of its authorship and context. We need not repeat that discussion here, even if it would be helpful to offer a brief summary of the matter to orient our more careful textual analysis of the narrative. We had mentioned that the narrative belongs to the "priestly voice", whose concerns are ritual and covenantal memory, and that this voice asserts itself most forcefully on the occasion of Israel's return from their forty-eight-year exile among the Babylonians. Thus, the main purpose of the present narrative is to re-establish Israel's cultural memory of the dogma of creation at the hands of the only God capable of creating—*Yahweh Elohim*: the God who is Love.

The ritualistic structure of the narrative is apparent in its emphasis upon a period of seven days, which provides a covenantal context within which to experience the sanctification of the calendar. Its literary configuration is intended to cast the whole structure of time and space in terms of God's ordered and intentional activity of love—what theologians call "providence"—and, thus, to depict an order of creation based on harmony rather than discord, and on love rather than hatred. The sanctification of time and space as deliberately created by Elohim means a cosmos imbued, from the very beginning, with meaning, purpose, and value rather than one cursed in its origins by futility, chaos, and inconsequence. This context thus supplies the framework for establishing a properly liturgical calendar, since time itself—our day-to-day life—is thoroughly bound-up with our understanding of God and creation. As we will see in our reading of this narrative, the text itself contains an explicit articulation of this principle.

That said, it is widely observed that the narrative involves obvious symmetry between the two halves of the week, with the seventh day representing a culminating, and even post-temporal event. That issue is essential in distinguishing this narrative from the *Enûma Elish*, the much older and considerably more primitive myth of origins that had circulated among Israel's former captors. In the Genesis account, the first day is mirrored in the fourth, the second in the fifth, and the third in the sixth, while the seventh day moves beyond mere creation, and enters upon the realm of worship in a decidedly Hebrew sense—that is to say, as *communion with God in love.* Thus, the narrative evinces the following structure:

Day 1:	Day 4:
God creates light.	God makes the heavenly lights.

Day 2:	Day 5:
God separates the abyss to make the heavens and the waters below.	God makes the water-dwelling animals and the birds of the air.

Day 3:	Day 6:
God brings forth dry land and makes it grow green with vegetation.	God makes the earth bring forth the beasts of the field and creates human beings, who will live on the land and eat the vegetation that grows upon it.

Day 7:
God draws creation back to himself, beyond the temporal cycle of coming-to-be and passing-away, and into the eternal dynamism of his own Love.

All of these elements demonstrate to the attentive reader just how much more sophisticated the Genesis narrative is in comparison with the rather bloated and clumsily-structured *Enûma Elish*. The Genesis narrative is tightly-woven, balanced, and rigorously economical. It is oriented to the communication of a specific dogmatic point, and to relating that point, in no uncertain terms, to the concrete ritual expression of covenant in the response of worship. Specific features of the *Enûma Elish* are referenced in the Genesis narrative, but are totally recast in the process.

For example, in the *Enûma Elish*, the first eon involves a reference to primordial formlessness, and to the waters of the abyss, just as does the first day in the Genesis narrative. In the case of the *Enûma Elish*, however, the waters of the abyss are the birth-place of the goddess Tiamat, who appears, as is typical for paganism, as a part of the cosmic structure. She becomes the mother deity, who gives birth to all other gods, but who, for her own part, is the personification of the primordial principle of evil and darkness. In the Genesis narrative, however, darkness is not depicted as a principle at all, but, instead, indicates only the emptiness of the uncreated being-void, of which the abyss, too, is symbolic, and over-against which God's spirit (*rua^ch Elohim* = רוּחַ אֱלֹהִים) hovers as the giver of being, form, light, and goodness.

In the *Enûma Elish*, the heavens, the earth, and the celestial bodies each appear in distinct episodes of the epic, just as they do in the Genesis narrative. The similarity here, however, is deliberately superficial. In the case of the *Enûma Elish*, the heavens, the earth, and the celestial bodies are the product of a cosmic conflagration, a great act of violence, conflict, and chaos in the realm of the gods, as Marduk tears his mother, Tiamat, limb from limb. Having agreed to overthrow her to secure freedom for his fellow gods in exchange for his own supremacy, he severs her head from her body, and casting it in one direction as her body flies off in another and her blood is shed far and wide, Marduk sees the material universe take shape as the precipitation of evil. In the Genesis narrative, by contrast, the universe is made intentionally by the only God there is, who, for his own part, totally transcends the cosmos that comes into being entirely at his command. In this narrative, the heavens, the earth, and the celestial bodies are each willed into existence from no pre-existing foundation, as an act of well-ordered love, resulting in a world that God sees as "very good."

Both the *Enûma Elish* and the Genesis narrative span *seven* distinct episodes. In the *Enûma Elish*, the cosmos gradually takes the shape of controlled chaos—evil dispersed and pitted against itself. In the Genesis narrative, however, the cosmos takes the shape of free order—goodness diffused in love. The result, in each case, is a seventh episode characterized in terms of a divine rest, but, once again, the similarities on this point are deliberately superficial. In the case of the *Enûma Elish*, human beings are made with the express purpose of personifying in countless individuals the power of evil that had once been centralized in the primordial personality of Tiamat, thus, leading to the enslavement of humanity as we serve the gods by keeping the cosmic structure in a cycle of balanced tension. In the case of the Genesis narrative, however, the seventh day involves the command that human beings rest from their labors, because God, having made us intentionally as the culmination of his entire creation—indeed, having made the entire cosmos for us from top to bottom—calls us to enter into the dialogue of love in which he exists for all eternity.

In the end, once again, the Genesis narrative of the seven days is presented to the People Israel as a direct confrontation with the Babylonian view of the universe, and, through it, with the whole pagan alternative to faith in Yahweh Elohim. It represents, then, a radical departure in perspective from paganism, and a powerful statement of the points on which paganism's basic error comes to grief against the truth about the world and the divine. It is a bold affirmation of the dogma of creation—a dogma that simply leaves no room at all for dualism, polytheism, or the notion that evil is a power of its own.

CHAPTER 4

✍

A Theological Interpretation of the Genesis Narrative

Fresh perspectives on classical texts call for fresh translations capable of drawing those perspectives out of the realm of mere theory and into the concreteness of our personal encounter with our original sources. Throughout our study, then, we have offered our own translations of the scriptural passages before us, and continue to do so as we turn, now, to the narrative of the seven days of creation in Genesis 1:1–2:4. Our purpose here is entirely theological, and we do not intend to digress into the purely exegetical details that form the basis of the contemporary critical methods of textual analysis, except insofar as attention to them might aid us in drawing out the theological content of the narrative. Approaching the narrative "one day at a time," so to speak, we will provide for each day of the narrative a few introductory remarks, our own translation of the text, and a brief analytical commentary. In some instances, we will also offer a "free translation" to help establish the sense of the text where the Hebrew does not lend itself easily to translation into English.

We cannot hope to be exhaustive in these pages, of course, but only to offer the reader an entrance into the text that takes account of the original theological concerns represented in the narrative. This task is worthwhile because these original theological concerns are taken up throughout the whole of the Bible, as central to the covenantal perspective of the People of God. This perspective is still relevant today, as the unifying element that constitutes what has come to be called the "Judeo-Christian tradition."

Day One

The first day of the Genesis narrative sets the stage for the whole theology of creation that we have been discussing so far in our study. As we have already said, the idea of creation finds its sole justification in the idea of God as *Elohim*. In fact, it is only imaginable at all on that basis, and in no way as a product of what Immanuel Kant would have referred to as "pure reason." To make this point plainly and unflinchingly is the main purpose of the narrative as a whole. In the discourse on the first day, in particular, the basic elements of this presentation are set before the reader. The passage reads:

> In the beginning, Elohim created the heavens and the earth.

The earth was formless and void, and darkness overlaid the surface of *abyss*—and the Spirit of Elohim was moving-gently upon the face of the waters. Elohim said, "Let there be light," and there was light; Elohim saw that the light was good. And Elohim separated the light from the darkness. Elohim called the light, "day," and the darkness he called, "night." Evening fell and morning broke: day one.[24]

The opening phrase of this discourse, "In the beginning, Elohim created," must certainly rank among the most important in the entire Bible, which, for its own part, stands, largely, as an elaboration on this theme. Certainly, John saw the matter this way as he set out to interpret the whole event of Christ in light of this narrative, and began his gospel by quoting directly from the text of Genesis 1:1, saying:

> In beginning was the *Logos*, and the *Logos* was together-with God, and a God-one was the *Logos*. This was in the beginning together-with God. All came to be through him, and, without him, nothing came to be.[25]

---

[24] Genesis 1:1–5.

[25] John 1:1–3. There can be no question here of John's deliberate intentions. He quotes not from the Hebrew but from the Greek Septuagint, which features a peculiar grammatical idiosyncrasy. In Greek, there are definite articles but not indefinite articles. One can say, "In *the* beginning," but must leave to context the work of determining the difference in meaning between, "In beginning" and "In a beginning." In any event, since the Hebrew *bərêšit* (בְּרֵאשִׁית) is commonly understood to indicate the singularity of the event, the Septuagint's reading of *en archë* (Ἐν ἀρχῇ), which lacks a definite article, is counter-intuitive. Yet, in spite of this difficulty, which an astute scholar such as John would certainly have understood, John chose to leave the Septuagint Greek he was quoting exactly as it appeared in the circulating manuscripts. This move shows that John regarded the Septuagint text as something more than a mere translation, and that he intended unquestionably to quote from Genesis

Indeed, in accord with John's reading of the essential truth of the Genesis narrative, we might even summarize the point further. "In the beginning, Elohim created," might be shortened to the essential revelation that makes for the whole: "In the beginning, Elohim."

We have already addressed the significance of this term for God, but it will emerge in this narrative as an indispensible interpretive element for the text as a whole. Furthermore, the idea of a God who is plural in his unity is the core intuition radicalized in the Christian dogma of the Trinity: wherein God is understood to subsist, essentially and from eternity, as three distinct but inseparable "persons", each of whom shares completely with the others, and in his totality, one and the same act of existence. To say that God is Elohim is to say that to be God is to be outwardly oriented, not self-referenced and self-enclosed. It means that to be God is to be truly infinite rather than constricted, and to be self-expansive rather than statically inert. This insight from the Judeo-Christian tradition most likely contributed to the neo-platonic assertion that "the Good is diffusive of itself," for this assertion comes from within the cultural and

---

1:1 in the prologue of his Gospel, presumably because he wanted the reader to understand the connection between the Christ event and the dogma of creation at the hands of Yahweh Elohim. This point is enhanced by the rather strange construction John employs when he leaves off the definite article in describing the divinity of the *Logos* (λόγοσ). We rendered this phrase "and a God-one was the *Logos*" in our translation. John does not mean to say, as the Jehovah's Witnesses wrongly suppose, that the *Logos* is not actually God, but, instead, that the *Logos* is a different "someone" of God from the Father. Later Trinitarian theology would express this mystery in much more refined and precise terms, saying that the *Logos* is *homoousios* (ὁμοούσιοσ) with the Father—of one and the same act of being. The Niceno-Constantinopolitan Creed reads, further on this point, "God from God, Light from Light, true God from true God, begotten not made."

historical context of the academic community of Alexandria in the time spanning from the second century BC through the third century AD, where Jewish and, later, Christian scholars helped shape the development of philosophy in late antiquity.

In any event, the dogmatic content of God as *Elohim* does lie at the root of the Christian dogma of the *Trinity*. From this point of view, in other words, the dogma of the Trinity must be seen to represent an authentically Hebrew conception of God, even if it is nowhere explicitly, or even consciously, suggested prior to the Christ-event.[26] The

---

[26] Philo of Alexandria (20 BC – 50 AD), however, the great Jewish Neo-Platonist, understood the number three as a correspondence to the inner power of God, and saw the *Logos* of God as the shaper of the material form of the world. He was, however, perhaps too heavily influenced in his own thinking by certain pagan elements of the Hellenistic philosophy he had, for his own part, helped to transform according to revelation. For in spite of his remarkable insights into the meaning of the scriptures, he could not fully perceive in them the dogmatic character of the idea of creation. It was not a matter of being unable to think the thought, in principle. Rather, he dismissed the idea of direct contact between the divine and his creature in a way reminiscent of pagan thought. Interestingly, this exact view became the center of Christianity's most formative dogmatic crisis, when the presbyter Arius of Alexandria denied the eternal divinity of the *Logos* on Philo's grounds that the creature could never bear directly the divine caress. He was condemned as a heretic at the First Council of Nicaea in 325. It was in this moment that the Catholic Church made clear for all time the absolute connection between the concept of Elohim (now seen under the revelation of the Trinity) and the idea of creation. The Church declared, emphatically, that the *Logos* of God is *homoousios* with the Father—of the same act of being—and that he does, in fact touch creation directly and in the unfathomable extreme. He creates us, and then penetrates our own form of existence to draw us back to himself again. This content has stood from that time as the hallmark of Christian orthodoxy—as the Church's concise articulation of the non-negotiable center of the Apostolic Faith.

Fathers of the Church, in any event, saw in the Genesis narrative a certain prefuguration of the Trinity, which they believed to be revealed definitively only in and through Jesus Christ. They understood that Christ's references to "God" are references particularly to the Person of the Father, and saw in this literary detail a decidedly Trinitarian picture of creation. In the beginning, the Father created the heavens and the earth, while the Holy Spirit gently-moved over the face of the waters, and God spoke his word—his *Logos* or his *Verbum* (as it had come to be translated into Latin in the Vulgate)—to impose being upon nothingness.

Once again, this notion of creation is a radical one in the ancient world. An absolutely transcendent God thinks and wills a world beyond himself. He *loves* the world into being, such that everything he creates is *good*. This pattern begins to emerge immediately in the narrative on the first day, when God creates "light."

Indeed, the significance of this image must not be under assessed. In the ancient typologies, "light" and "darkness" were indications of the dual principles of "good" and "evil." By beginning their narrative with the creation of light, the priestly authors are making explicit the fact that belief in Elohim leaves no room for a dualistic view of the universe. It is only in this way—only because he is Elohim—that God can truly "separate the light from the darkness."

The wording of the discourse is clear. With no words at their disposal to articulate the profound metaphysical point they are attempting to make for the first time in the ancient world, the authors choose familiar typological images indicative of *nothingness*, and, by linking other familiar typological images representative of evil to those representative of nothingness, paint the picture of God's unitary creative initiative, according to which the God who is Love is the author of all there is, and evil has no positive being of its own. This point is made more explicit, still, in the fact that God has named the light *yom* (יוֹם = *warmth* or *comfort*) and the darkness *la'yilh* (לַיְלָה = *a twisting-away*). Once again, "light", representative of positive goodness, is truly "separated" from the "darkness", which, for its own part, has its only reality as a "twisting-away" from the *yom*—from the *warmth* and *comfort* of God's love.

It seems fairly certain, as well, that the Hebrew word *tehom* (תְּהוֹם = *abyss*) is related to the Old Babylonian name for the goddess *Tiamat* (a name that also means "abyss" or "sea") and that it is used here as a direct reference to that figure, but now in a completely depersonalized form. We no longer face the terrifying power of a personal presence in the form of the goddess Tiamat, but only the impersonal nothingness of *tehom*, over-against which God simply asserts his creative will. The term appears in the Hebrew without a definite article, in this case, not because it is *someone*, like Tiamat, but because it is nothing at all—it is a privation of love.

Taking another look at the discourse on the first day, then, we might offer what people used to call a "free translation," in which we attempt to arrive at the underlying *sense* of the text. From this point of view, it would read:

> In the beginning, Elohim created the heavens and the earth. Rather than the earth, there was formlessness and void, and *abyss* was overlaid in darkness—and over-against this emptiness, the Spirit of Elohim moved-caressingly. Elohim said, "Let there be light," and there was light; Elohim saw that the *light* was *good*. And Elohim separated the *light* from the *darkness*. Elohim called

the light, "warmth" or "comfort," and the darkness he called, "a twisting-away." Evening fell and morning broke: day one.[27]

Thus, we see that the creation narrative of the priestly voice begins with a profoundly optimistic view of the universe, quite unlike anything affirmed by Israel's neighboring cultures. The narrative even includes two repeating emphases on this theme of uncompromising optimism. The first is in the phrase, "Elohim saw that it was good," indicating that only goodness is the product of creation, and only goodness, therefore, possesses positive power. The second is in the phrase, "evening fell and morning broke," which stresses the rhythm of time in the Hebrew consciousness. By emphasizing the Hebrew manner of dating the calendar with the fall of evening, the authors remind the reader that the whole rhythm of time in Elohim's creation possesses a positive trajectory. It is, as theologians have come to say, "*eschatological*."

We should comment a bit more on this last point, since it comes to represent, not only a central theme in the present narrative but also a central theme in the Bible as a whole, and in the universal consciousness of the Judeo-Christian tradition. The world is headed somewhere. Time is not, as it is in the pagan religions, merely cosmic self-repetitions. Even if it is the case—and we insist that it is—that, in the biblical worldview, time spirals over itself again and again, it must be said that it is always spiraling upward, and in an ever-tightening spool, until, finally, the whole of creation arrives at a definitive fulfillment.

We will have to return to this theme later, when we treat the seventh day, in which God inaugurates the Sabbath. For

---

[27] Genesis 1:1–5.

now, however, we should say that, if the day begins when it is dark, and moves forward into light—if emptiness is impressed with the divine presence—then the world is getting better as it comes more fully into being. The idea of creation, then, involves the paradoxical concept of a world that draws ever-nearer to God in its coming-forth from him. This perspective is represented in the book of Revelation, where we see a world so radically illuminated by the divine presence that, "the city [the heavenly Jerusalem] has no need of a sun, nor of a moon, that they might shine upon it, for the glory of God is its light, and its lamp is the lamb."[28] Paul, too, reflects on this image, when he says that, "God will be all-in-all."[29] The Christian notion of the *Parousia* (παρουσία), which, following upon the actual meaning of the Greek term, indicates God's, "placing himself intimately near to us by his face-to-face presence," belongs entirely to the optimism that runs through the whole of the Bible from the first chapter of Genesis to the last chapter of the book of Revelation.

Day two

The second day in the creation narrative involves the separation of the abyss between "above" and "below" for the formation of the skies or "heavens". This concept (the "heavens") is not to be understood strictly as the abode of God, although the fact that there are not two words for "skies" and "heavens" reminds us of just how novel the Hebrew conception of God and cosmos really were in their

---

[28] Revelation 21:23.

[29] Cf. 1 Corinthians 15:28.

historical context. Once again, the ancient pagans saw the gods as, somehow or other, bound into the cosmic frame. They had their proper dwelling place in some sphere above the ground on which we stand, somewhere high up in the sky, above the clouds, which they could inhabit in their rarefied, spiritual forms. For example, in the Babylonian myth of the *Enûma Elish*, the barrier of the heavens is a set of bars designed to hold back the waters of chaos surging forth from one half of the dismembered body of the evil dragon goddess Tiamat, once she is defeated by her son, Marduk. Once again, Tiamat is the goddess of chaos and evil—the goddess of the abyss—so a space for the other gods is secured, only upon her death, and only when her body is torn asunder. The gods live in the space between the waters. The partition of the heavens, then, in the Babylonian myth, is formed in the hopes of carving out a space for the gods between the two "waters" of Tiamat's body: those above and those below, where those below are the stuff of the earth.

Here again, the Genesis narrative moves in an entirely different direction from the *Enûma Elish*. Elohim does not live in the heavens. He does not seek to carve out a space for himself between the boundaries imposed upon the life of the spirit by the power of death. The God of the Bible transcends the bounds of everything that is born and dies. He stands completely beyond the cosmic frame. In this aspect, no other spiritual being conceived in the pagan cultures of the ancient world could lay claim to the sort of divinity Elohim enjoys. Whatever may live upon or within the firmament of the sky, however rarified its form, it is limited and subject to the power of the God who is Love. This is the context in which the discourse on the second day is to be understood. We read, there:

> Elohim said, "Let there be an expanse in the midst of the waters, [so] the waters become divided-between." Elohim made the expanse, and divided-between: between the waters which were beneath the expanse [and] the waters which were upon the expanse; and it was, just-so. Elohim proclaimed the expanse, "heavens." Evening fell and morning broke: day two.[30]

Once again, in this discourse, the authors exploit the typological image of "the waters of the abyss," just as they had in the discourse on the first day, to draw attention to God's absolute sovereignty in his creative action. This symbol for the power of sin and death—that which can swallow up the person and make him disappear—now becomes a symbol for God's power *over* sin and death: for the fact that he alone determines how far sin and death may have their effect. He has *divided* the waters between themselves, imposed limits upon them, and constrained them; but no one has been killed, and no one has been torn asunder.

A "free translation" of the passage in question might, then, be rendered thusly:

> Elohim said, "Let there be, in the midst of the waters, a partition to come between them and divide them from within." Elohim made this partition, dividing the waters from within. It was just that way: a severance of the waters beneath the partition from the waters that rest upon the partition. Elohim proclaimed the partition, "heavens." Evening fell and morning broke: day two.[31]

In this rendering of the passage in question, we attempt to capture the sense of the typology employed by the priestly

---

[30] Genesis 1:6–8.

[31] Genesis 1:6–8.

authors. The waters, here a symbol of sin and death, are sundered from within—broken up and kept apart—by a force generated from the divine will. The reader will note that the actual sense of the image of the partition—what has frequently been called a "firmament"—is a kind of floor upon which a portion of the waters now rests, as if somehow pressing center-ward on an inverted bowl or dome, high above the surface of the ground. This image represents the limitations God places upon the abyss, such that creation is characterized not by the inescapable power of death, but, instead, by the proliferation of life through love.

Day Three

The third day of the narrative involves the emergence of life in God's creation. God commands the earth to bring forth vegetation—material organisms capable of self-propagation. One will note that it is also on "the third day" that Christ rises from the dead, bringing life to the garden in which he had been laid upon his death. This detail of the resurrection is important because, in the logic of the Incarnation, the death of Christ involves a breaking-down of the barrier between the world of the living and the world of the dead. It means, in other words, a reversal of what had happened on the third day of creation—that the abyss, having been divided still further beneath the heavens, made a space for life. When, with our rejection of the Living God, the world of the living now collapses, once again, into "the abyss," the dead come to walk among the living.[32] But, as this very event already indicates, the breaking-down of this

---

[32] Matthew 27:52.

barrier will not mean, in the end, what it appears to mean at first, as the Apostles lock themselves in the upper room, fearing for what remains of their lives. In the resurrection, "on the third day," God will bring life into the world once more, even for the dead.

The relationship between the resurrection logic of the New Testament and the original context of the discourse on the third day is clear, once we understand the fact that both events revolve around the problem of life in relation to death. Indeed, the Fathers of the Church understood this parallel very clearly. Ambrose, for example, commenting on the discourse on the third day of creation, explains that, "whatever has been sown rises again in its own nature. . . [such] that flesh is restored from flesh, bone from bone, blood from blood, the humours of the body from humours."[33] Gregory of Nyssa, likewise, declares:

> [W]e learn from Scripture in the account of the first creation, that first the earth brought forth "the green herb" (as the narrative says), and that then from this plant seed was yielded, from which, when it was shed on the ground, the same form of the original plant again sprang up. . . and so we learn . . . not only that our humanity will be then changed into something nobler, but also that what we have therein to expect is nothing else than that which was at the beginning.[34]

---

[33] Ambrose, *On Belief in the Resurrection*, 2.70, in, Philip Schaff, D.D., LL.D. and Henry Wace, D.D., eds. *A Select Library of the Nicene and Post Nicene Fathers of the Christian Church*, Series 2 (New York: The Christian Literature Company, 1896),Vol. 10:185.

[34] Gregory of Nyssa, *On the Soul and the Resurrection*, in *Nicene and Post-Nicene Fathers*, Series 2, Vol. 5:467. Gregory's theology is truly fascinating, and represents a perspective, which, however widely held in the early Church, has been almost completely forgotten in our own

So, returning to our consideration of the narrative's original context, we should remember, once again, that among the governing directives of the priestly authors is that of staking out the radical difference between the Hebrew view of the universe and that of their former captors in Babylon. The contrasts are stark, indeed, for, while the Judeo-Christian tradition stresses the generosity and life-giving love of God (leading, by the first century BC, to a widespread belief in personal immortality and resurrection), the Babylonians see a world constrained within the boundaries imposed by death, boundaries that cannot be surmounted.

In the Epic of Gilgamesh, for example, which belongs to the Babylonian tradition, our hero embarks upon a quest in search of the secret of eternal life, only to learn that it is denied him. The gods have chosen to hoard life for themselves alone, and Gilgamesh must be content to find his consolation in the here and now. Having traveled across the abyss, and amidst "the waters of death," he could find no final promise of life at the end of his journey, nor should he

---

time. Gregory goes on, in the text cite here, to develop a theology of resurrection based upon the idea of a primordial Adam—a collective humanity—who, on account of his sin, was dispersed into mere multiplicity from his original organismic communion, such that, in Christ the New Adam, the totality of the primordial Adam is restored. This approach, taken also by St. Augustine, avoids the major theological difficulties concerning contemporary theories of evolution in the context of the doctrine of "original sin" as a kind of "privative inheritance" from a single set of first parents in whom the whole of humanity was primordially implicated. The basic contours of this view are also articulated by Origen in the early third century, and much more recently by theologians such as Teilhard de Chardin and Joseph Ratzinger (who sees Teilhard as offering a fundamentally correct reading of St. Paul on the point in question [Joseph Ratzinger, *Introduction to Christianity*, 177]).

have expected one. For, this image of the abyss—of the ocean—is, in itself, the image of death. Gilgamesh could not escape "the waters of death," no matter how careful he was to avoid them, for they are the stuff of the cosmos itself.

From the Babylonian context, this sad tale of humanity's seemingly futile aspirations makes perfect sense. For, again, the image of the abyss is related, in their literature, to the dragon goddess Tiamat: the primordial mother goddess, the personification of chaos and evil in the *Enûma Elish*. When her children in the pantheon rise up against her, the world of our experience begins to emerge. Her son, Marduk, dismembers and disembowels her, her body is divided, and her crushed head is cast away into the outer darkness.

Since Tiamat is representative of the chaos and evil of the abyss, it is clear that the biblical narrative introduces a familiar choreography but with entirely different actors, and with an entirely different meaning. In the discourse on the third day in the Genesis narrative, God does not have to destroy anything that the world might take its shape, much less rely upon primordially evil raw materials. The earth is not formed out of any portion of the divided body of *Tiamat*, even though it is the case, in the Genesis narrative, that dry land appears when the *abyss* has been divided, and now divided again. The authors are deliberately referencing the archetypes employed in the *Enûma Elish*, but purifying them and employing them in a way that shows Elohim's singular and intentional action in the formation of the world on the paradigm of his own love, with no suggestion of violence anywhere in the narrative.

Turning, then to the passage in question, we may read the discourse on the third day as follows:

> Elohim said, "Let the waters beneath the heavens be detained in one area [and] the dryness show forth." And it was, just-so: Elohim proclaimed the dryness, "earth", and the gathering-together of the waters he proclaimed, "seas". And Elohim saw that it was good. Elohim said, "Let the earth grow green with grass, with vegetation bearing seed, and with fruit trees developing fruit bearing seed for their own kind on the earth." And it was, just-so: the earth grew green with grass, with vegetation bearing seed, and with fruit trees developing fruit bearing seed for their own kind. Elohim saw that it was good. Evening fell and morning broke: day three.[35]

Now, the reader will note that, in this discourse, God commands life to emerge from within the earth itself. The earth "grows green with grass," and other vegetation. This pattern will be repeated on days five and six, when God commands animal life of all kinds to appear. A difference will appear in the discourse on day six, only when God seeks to make human beings, and we will speak at length about that matter when we deal directly with that text. In the mean time, we should be prepared to accept that the Genesis narrative suggests a biological paradigm likely to surprise a reader of our own time. The biological paradigm of the Genesis narrative is one in which life emerges from within the material structure of the world—a biology in which the world simply erupts with life. We must not forget, of course, that it does so according to the divine command (a fact upon which the Fathers of the Church were absolutely insistent), but we should also be prepared to accept that, according to this model, the living things of the earth (up to the creation of human beings, in any case) appear only as various stages in the unfolding of an order of creation brought about in an

---

[35] Genesis 1:11–13.

original and singular act. In other words, the text makes very clear that the real moment of creation occurs on the first day, when God wills there to be something other than himself rather than the void of nothingness. In what follows after that point, what God has willed into existence now takes the shape he coaxes out of it. Both events require the direct influence of God, but only the first is *creation* in the proper sense.

Once we understand the text in this light, we can avoid a great deal of needless controversy with contemporary science. There is nothing at stake for the faith in the idea that matter comes, by stages, to be organized in ways that ultimately take the shape of life. That thesis is already anticipated by the Genesis account, and it was more or less widely accepted as a biological paradigm throughout the Middle Ages, as we can see in some rather odd-seeming hypotheses about the relationship between certain types of animals and their natural habitats. For example, even in Christendom, people once thought that frogs emerged spontaneously out of mud puddles, and fish materialized out of the waters of the ocean. Although we now know that these hypotheses are incorrect, they provided the original basis for distinguishing cold-blooded meat from warm-blooded meat for the sake of the abstinence rubrics in the Catholic Church. The flesh of these sorts of animals did not contribute to "the excitement of the passions," because those animals—then thought neither male nor female—were not spawned in connection with any passionate movement.

All of this goes to make a basic point: contemporary scientists would do well to adopt a broader understanding of the history of thought, and to understand, on that basis, that there is nothing in the thesis of the *biologization* of matter (matter organizing itself into living forms) as such that

Christian faith cannot accept. The problem emerges only once we insist that God is not the principal agent in this movement—a claim that, in any event, natural science can neither affirm nor deny from within its own methodological framework. When people of faith come to understand that the Genesis narrative itself describes a process of material biologization, and natural scientists recognize that their methodology does not allow them to draw conclusions about supernatural causes for this process, one way or another, we will finally be able to focus upon the real issues that lie beneath the controversy, and beneath the text of the Bible. It is not a question of what natural scientific theories can describe, but a question of one's basic attitude toward the fundamental meaning and value of the cosmos: do we accept that the world is founded on love—is loved into being by *Elohim*—or not?

Day Four

The events of the fourth day in the Genesis narrative correspond, roughly, to the events of the fifth tablet—the fifth eon—in the Babylonian narrative of the *Enûma Elish*. Nonetheless, apart from the fact that both narratives involve the formation of the celestial bodies, the two expressions represent radically different, and, indeed, opposing interpretations of their significance. In the *Enûma Elish*, the formation of the celestial bodies serves the gods who have survived the great struggle against Tiamat. They are a part of the home of the gods, separated from the earth, which, on the previous tablet, had been formed out of a portion of Tiamat's dismembered corpse. We should also note that the fertility of the earth depends upon Tiamat's saliva, dripping down, in the form of rain, through the heavens from the outer darkness into which her crushed head had been thrust by Marduk's vanquishing hand. The whole material world, once again, is presented here as an evil and wretched place—an abomination from which the gods seek to barricade themselves in a sphere of their own.

The Genesis narrative, however, represents an entirely different point of view than that expressed in the *Enûma Elish*, and the discourse on the fourth day makes that fact clear by declaring that the celestial bodies are not meant to carve out a protected space for the gods, but to forge a link between God and human beings. It is for this reason that the formation of the celestial bodies, in the numerical logic of the narrative structure of this myth, must occur on the fourth day, not on the fifth.

The fourth day is the first day of the second half of the week. It should be read, therefore, over-against the first day. This day represents the stage in which God comes into contact with the world of human beings. Even though human beings do not yet exist in the context of the narrative, the narrative shows the movement of light from the realm of abstraction to the realm of the concrete. Particularizing "light" in the form of the sun, the moon, and the stars, God sets these lights in the heavens, but he sets them there that they might "become-light upon the earth."

The fourth day, therefore, must be regarded as an immensely significant stage in this narrative. It stands in the present context just as the fourth commandment ("Honor your father and your mother") stands in the context of the Decalogue. As the first commandment of the second tablet, it reaffirms and makes concrete our initial affirmation of God in the first commandment of the first tablet. In this way, the fourth commandment provides the essential link between the concerns of the two tablets, and we come to understand that we can only really fulfill our obligations toward God inasmuch as we affirm our fellow human beings. This is what Christ means, when he says that the first and greatest commandment is the love of God above all things, while the second is "in its likeness": that we would love our neighbor as another self.[36] Here, in other words, Christ sees all the commandments of the law to be distilled in the interrelationship between the concerns of the two tablets, and he makes that very claim, explicitly, declaring that, "on these, the two commandments, the whole law hangs, and the prophets."[37]

The discourse on the fourth day serves a purpose like this one. It helps us to understand that God does not create merely that something else might exist, but that his creation might return to him again in love. The fourth day brings the light at the dawn of creation into the lives of human beings, who will find in the celestial bodies, "indicators for festivals, days, and years." Only human beings care about these things, because only human beings mark the passage of time, conscious of their own contingency and finitude in the tension of their aspirations to transcendence, and only human beings ask the question about the relationship between themselves and the world around them. The fourth day reminds us that we cannot understand the meaning of human life apart from the dogma of creation, and that we cannot understand the dogma of creation apart from the mystery of God's love for human beings—the mystery, that is to say, of "election."

With this context in mind, then, we might translate the passage as follows:

---

[36] Matthew 22:39.

[37] Matthew 22:40.

Elohim said, "Let there come to be lights in the partition of the heavens to divide-between: between the "day" and the "night." Let them come to be as indicators for festivals, days, and years. Let them come to be as lights in the partition of the heavens, to become-light upon the earth." And it was, just-so. Elohim made the two great lights—the greater light to govern the day, and the lesser light to govern the night—and the stars. Elohim placed them in the partition of the heavens to become-light upon the earth, to govern the day and the night, and to divide-between: the light from the darkness. Elohim saw that it was good. Evening fell and morning broke: day four.[38]

Once again, the fourth day holds immense significance within this narrative. It marks the central episode in the account, and it brings into view the whole thrust of the biblical revelation. Indeed, there can be no question that John, in the prologue of his Gospel, interprets the fourth day precisely as we have already described it—as the point of intersection between the abstract and the concrete, and, thus, as an indication of the movement of the divine Love as Elohim pours himself out for his creation, that we might return to him some day, and share in his life. John illustrates this point when he says that, "What had come to be in him was true-life and the true-life was the light of human beings; and the light shines in the darkness; and the darkness did not constrain it."[39] Through the relationship between the first and the fourth days of the Genesis narrative, John sees the whole movement of creation as an in-breaking of God upon the cosmos.

John, to make the point another way, sees God to have begun the process of entering into his creation from the very

---

[38] Genesis 1:14–19.

[39] John 1:4–5.

first moment in which he loved it into being. The evangelist makes this point when he draws out a four-stage movement of God's penetration into creation, starting with his depiction of the *Logos* of God (who becomes Incarnate as Jesus of Nazareth) as the *exemplar* of the light that God creates in the beginning. This exemplar is the "true light," which constitutes the *logos* by which the created light is to be measured and understood. But, just as the created light is given over to human beings, moving beyond the partition of the heavens "to become-light upon the earth," so the "true light" moves from beyond the heavens—from "the bosom of the Father"[40]—into the human heart. This is what John means, when he writes, "He was the true light, who enlightens all humanity, coming into the cosmos. He was in the cosmos . . . . He came to his own . . . .and the *Logos* became flesh, and tented within us."[41] Ratzinger sums up what he sees as the central point of the whole dogma of creation—its inner logic, to which John attempts to give expression—saying, "God created the universe in order to be able to become a human being and pour out his love upon us and to invite us to love him in return."[42]

Now, John's language, if we might return to it for a moment, also brings out another important dimension of the creation narrative as it concerns the discourse on the fourth day. We should remember, once again, that the fourth day is related to the first day, where God created light and "separated the light from the darkness." In the end, as we

---

[40] John 1:18.

[41] John 1:9, 1:11, 1:14.

[42] Joseph Ratzinger, *'In the Beginning': A Catholic Understanding of the Story of Creation and the Fall*, Boniface Ramsey, O.P., trans. (Grand Rapids, Michigan: William B. Eerdmans Publishing Company, 1995), 30.

have said, this separation means that creation does not emerge from two distinct and opposing principles, but from a single principle of origin: God himself. We had said that rooting the origin of all things in Elohim—the only God capable of thinking and willing something other than himself—means that evil or "darkness" is not strictly necessary for the world, but has its reality only as a privation; it can only be at all as *la'yilh* (לַיְלָה): "a twisting-away" from the love of Elohim.

What this ultimately means is now expressed, in the discourse on the fourth day, in the figures of the greater and lesser lights, and the stars. In the universe created by God—loved into being by Elohim—there is no such thing as total darkness. Since, in other words, darkness possesses no positive existence at all, it can only make itself present as a diminishment of light. This means that the light, for its own part, can never be completely extinguished, but always breaks through "the partition of the heavens" to make itself present on the earth. The images employed by the priestly authors in their discourse on the fourth day, therefore, show a world defined, not by darkness but by light: not by evil but by good, not by death but by life, not by sin but by grace. Even to the extent that "day" gives way to "night," it maintains its absolute authority in creation, because "the lesser light" (the moon) still governs, even in this moment. Indeed, even when this "lesser light" goes completely dark in the sky for one night each month, the stars remain in the heavens to keep order in the night. "The light," as John says, "shines in the darkness; indeed, the darkness did not constrain it."[43]

---

[43] John 1:5.

This insight from the creation narrative becomes the inner logic behind what the Fathers of the Church would describe as "the harrowing of hell"—Christ's penetration of the darkness of death all the way to the very bottom of the abyss, "to its darkest, deepest place,"[44] where the light of the divine life now shines through and "dispels the darkness of sin,"[45] leading to restoration and resurrection. This mystery is expressed, liturgically, in the context of the Easter Vigil, which reveals the positive salvific content of Holy Saturday. We learn, in the opening actions of the Vigil liturgy, that even in the silence of the preceding day, when Christ lay cold in his tomb, life still reigned over death. The glimmering of the stars punctured the shroud of the ultimate Night, as God's creation, in the ultimate act of futility, had "cast him into the outer darkness,"[46] ensuring his presence to everyone who "goes down into the dust of death."[47] This is why the readings for the Easter Vigil liturgy begin with the creation narrative in Genesis and continue all the way to the resurrection; and it is why the liturgy begins after dark, with the kindling of a fire and the lighting of a candle.

Day Five

The discourse on the fifth day is characterized by the transformation of the abyss from an image of death to an image of life. It foreshadows the story of the great flood

---

[44] Psalm 88:6b.

[45] Exultet.

[46] Cf. Matthew 25:30.

[47] Cf. Psalm 22:15, and also, Zephaniah 1:17, Amos 2:7, Psalm 44:25, Psalm 88:3–7, and Isaiah 51:23.

(which certainly takes its context from this narrative) and the ritual of baptism, which, adopted by the Essenes shortly before the advent of Christ would be taken up into Christianity in the form of a sacrament. Paul takes note of this meaning of baptism and its relation to the idea that the regenerated Christian is "a new creation."[48] He asks the faithful, "Do you not know that as many as were baptized into Christ Jesus were baptized into his death?"[49] And he explains that, "We were buried together with him through the baptism into the death, so that just as Christ, indeed, through the glory of the Father, got up from [being] dead, so also we might walk-about in newness of true-life."[50]

In the discourse on the fifth day, we have seen the nothingness of the abyss divided from itself, and divided from itself again, until now, God is able to command that it be filled with living things. Indeed, the Hebrew words employed at this stage in the narrative make the point with a clarity that cannot be reproduced in the English language. We can attempt a translation as follows:

> Elohim said, "Let the waters teem with swarms of living things. Let birds fly above the earth, on the face of the partition of the heavens." Elohim made the great dragons, and every living thing that moves about, that swarmed the waters in their kind, and every kind of winged bird. Elohim saw that it was good. Elohim blessed them, saying, "Be fruitful and become many. Fill the waters and the seas; birds, become many upon the earth." Evening fell and morning broke: day five.[51]

---

[48] 2 Corinthians 5:17.
[49] Romans 6:3.
[50] Romans 6:4.
[51] Genesis 1:20–23.

It is not possible, however, to translate the Hebrew *neh'fesh hahayah* (נֶפֶשׁ הַחַיָּה) in any way that really makes sense in English. We have translated these words here as, "living things," but the word *neh'fesh* (נֶפֶשׁ) does not really mean "things." The term is sometimes translated as "creatures," but this is only because, in English, we tend to associate the word "creatures" with animals of various types, rather than with inanimate objects. The concept being communicated in the Hebrew is not exactly the same as this, and it cannot be translated into any meaningfully cognate English terms. It is *emphatically redundant*, in the way that the English expressions "diametrically opposed" and "young children" are emphatically redundant. The Hebrew phrase can be translated more or less as, "living livings", which makes little sense in English, but which is meant to communicate the idea of animal life as something distinct from vegetable life. Animals are more fully alive—more perfectly differentiated from the merely material world than plant life is. They move around on their own; they express desire, respond to stimuli, feel pleasure and pain, fight to preserve their lives, and flee dangers they imagine they can avoid. They can also be domesticated, responding to the commands of human beings, and conforming their behavior to our ends. The discourse on the fifth day involves the emergence of this sort of life.

The reader will note, also, that the discourse on the fifth day includes an indirect reference to the Babylonian goddess Tiamat, in the phrase, "Elohim made the great dragons." Recalling, once again, that Tiamat is the dragon goddess of the abyss, and that the meaning of this phrase in the context of the present narrative is something akin to "sea-dragons", it is clear that the authors had in mind a reference to the Babylonian goddess. They meant to say that the gods of their pagan neighbors were no true gods at all in comparison to Elohim. If they existed, they existed just as we do: as creatures of Elohim. Thus, there is no "goddess of the abyss," and the waters in Elohim's creation are not the waters of chaos, as in the *Enûma Elish* of the Babylonians, but the waters of life—the waters of abundance and grace.

We will see this truth force its way into our awareness again and again in the pages of the Bible, as water becomes the means of renewal, the vehicle of restoration, the avenue of escape, the signifier of God's providence, etc. It is no coincidence, for example, that the narrative of the Red Sea Crossing in the Book of Exodus,[52] involves the images of God's spirit moving over the waters, dividing the abyss of the sea and "establishing a desert out of the sea."[53] Here we see that, "the sons of Israel went by the dryness into the midst of the sea,"[54] passing from death in pagan Egypt to life in the presence of God. Throughout the Bible, the typology of water undergoes this very transformation, such that what at first appears as the darkness of death might be transmuted before our eyes into the life-giving love of God.

For Peter, nowhere is this fact clearer than in the case of the story about Noah and the Ark. With penetrating insight, Peter sees, through the lens of Christ's death and resurrection, that even the Noah's ark story is not really about God's desire to destroy the wicked—something God explicitly tells us he does not wish to do[55]—but about his

---

[52] Exodus 14:1–15:21.

[53] Cf. Exodus 14:21.

[54] Exodus 14:22.

[55] Cf. Ezekiel 33:11, "Utter into-their-midst: 'I live,' says the Lord Yahweh, '[I] take no delight in the death of the wicked, but [in] that he return from his wicked wandering and live,'" and Hosea 11:8b–9: "The wholeness of my compassions heats up! I will not act on my

uncompromising intention to save them. For Peter, the Noah's ark story means that God is even more intractable than we are—even more unyielding in his pursuit of the sinner than the sinner is in the will to be lost. We attempt, here, to allow Peter to speak, as much as possible, for himself as he writes, in a passage that, for all its power and profundity, simply resists an English translation:

> Christ, in a singular instance, suffered for sins—righteous for unrighteous—that he might bring us to God. Having been put to death, indeed, in flesh, but having been made truly-alive in spirit, and, in which [that is, in spirit], having made his way to the spirits in prison, he preached-to-persuade [those who,] having refused to conform [to God] sometime [ago], in the days of God's patient-waiting, when Noah was building the ark into which few—that is, eight souls—were delivered through water, which also prefigures the baptism which saves us now: not a putting-down of the spreading-filth of flesh, but a response in good conscience to God [as he poses a question] by the resurrection of Jesus Christ, who is God's right hand, having made his way to heaven, angels having been placed under his authority, along with those of position and those of power.
> . . . . You have been proceeding along the pagans' planned route for enough time: taking your course of life in debaucheries, unbridled desires, states of insobriety, carousings, episodes of binge-drinking, and illicit acts of worship before idols. In this, they think it strange, your not running along with them in this same wantonness [which is] flooding-out, blaspheming [along with them], who will return an account to the one who takes it upon himself readily to stand in [divine] judgment over truly-living and dead. For this reason, the good-news was delivered to

---

burning rage! I will not destroy Ephraim again, for I am the Divine, not a mere human male, the Holy One in your midst, and I am-not-one-to come in terror!"

the dead also, that although they might, indeed, face the judgment of humanity in flesh, they might truly-live by God in spirit.[56]

The important point for our purposes is the fact that Peter has correctly intuited, and, in the context of the New Testament, witnessed directly to, the paradoxical meaning of the abyss typology as it appears in the Bible. Our first indication of this paradoxical meaning is found in the creation narrative as it moves through the stages of the first, third, and fifth days. The abyss itself becomes an environment of life, when God says, "Let the waters team with swarms of living things."

Day Six

The sixth day is the day on which God brings into being both land-dwelling animals and human beings. One might wonder why God performs both of these acts on the same day. Why does he not bring the beasts into being on one day, and create human beings on another? There is, after all, another day still to pass in the narrative. Perhaps, one might suggest, this is an argument in favor of a diminished understanding of human beings on the part of the priestly authors in contrast to the exalted view of humanity typically ascribed to them. Maybe they mean to say that human beings are really no better than the beasts. After all, if humanity is the fulfillment of creation, why not create us on the day of fulfillment, the *seventh* day?

This question cannot be answered apart from the discourse on the seventh day, of course, because it is only in that narrative that we come to understand the manner in

---

[56] 1 Peter 3:18–22, 4:3–6.

which humanity becomes, definitively, the fulfillment of the world. In the mean time, we are left with an incomplete account of both humanity and the cosmos. The priestly authors, however, intend this very thing, for the number six in Jewish numerology—what the rabbis have called, "*gematria*" (גימטריה)—means, "near fulfillment." It appears, for example, in the Cana narrative in John's Gospel,[57] where Jesus turns the water of ritual cleansing into covenantal wine, though his "hour has not yet come."[58] He performs this miracle using "six stone water-pots."[59]

It is paradoxical, then, that the authors deviate at this point from their previous phrasing, according to which each day is punctuated by a *cardinal* number: "day one," "day two," etc. In the case of the sixth day, this punctuation is altered, and an *ordinal* number, with a definite article, is used instead: "the sixth day." This phraseology indicates that the sixth day stands apart from the rest—that it represents some momentous and defining event. According to a strong current of interpretation represented both by ancient Jewish commentators and certain Fathers of the Church, "the sixth day" was the present time—the age in which we live now, which yet awaits fulfillment in a stage of development not yet fully realized. This line of interpretation, which would allow for concepts like, "the day of the Lord," "the day of mercy," and "the day of judgment," meant that each Sabbath day in our lived experience would have to be understood as a participation in time of a reality still beyond the horizon of this world.

---

[57] John 2:1–12.

[58] John 2:3.

[59] John 2:4.

Whether we see "the sixth day" in that light or not—that is, as a representation of the present stage of history within which we live out our lives—the basic lines of that interpretation remain more or less valid. The sixth day needs the seventh; for, the Sabbath day will bring creation to fulfillment and give both humanity and the whole of creation its true meaning and value. Furthermore, there can be no question that the concrete Sabbath day in time is to be understood as a reality opened up beyond itself to eternity. In any event, we should remember that the Sabbath day had already been anticipated on the fourth day, when God set the celestial bodies in the heavens to be "indicators for festivals, days, and years."[60] Throughout the whole of the Genesis narrative, God is making the world for human beings, but he makes human beings for love; so, the Sabbath day must be forged into the whole structure of the cosmos from the very beginning. The sixth day is the final stage in the creation of the cosmos, but it is not the final stage in God's love for us.

In the end, then, while we yet await the *seventh* day of this narrative, the *sixth* day should be understood to communicate four main points. First, God makes everything in the universe, without exception; second, human beings are not made by God in the same way as other things, but are made to be different and to be more fully blessed; third, femininity is not evil; and, fourth, God is provident for the needs of his creatures.

All four of these insights are profoundly significant in the context of the ancient world, because none of them could be taken for granted in the pagan context. All four of these points, therefore, mark out the discourse on the sixth day as

---

[60] Genesis 1:14.

unequivocally Hebrew—as belonging uniquely to the Judeo-Christian tradition. We translate it as follows:

> Elohim said, "Let there emerge from the earth living things by their kind: beasts and creeping things—[things] of the earth alive by their kind." And it was, just-so. Elohim made the living of the earth by their kind: the beasts in their kind, and every species that creeps upon the ground.
>
> Elohim said, "Let us accomplish-the-mighty-act [of] humanity in our image: according to our likeness. Let them have dominion over the fish of the sea, the birds of the heavens, all the beasts of the earth, and every creeping thing that creeps upon the earth."
>
> > Elohim created humanity in his [own] image;
> > in the image of Elohim he created them:
> > male and female he created them.
>
> Elohim blessed them; Elohim said, "Be fruitful, become many, fill the earth, and subject it to your authority. Exercise dominion over the fish of the sea, the birds of the heavens—[over] every living thing that moves upon the earth."
>
> Elohim said, "Aaah! I have given: all vegetation yielding seed that is on the face of the whole earth, and every tree that has fruit; every tree yielding seed shall become food. For all the living of the earth—[for] every bird of the heavens and everything that creeps upon the earth that is a living thing—green herbs [are their] food." And it was, just-so. Elohim saw all that he had made: "Aaah! Very good!" Evening fell and morning broke: the sixth day.[61]

If we return, once again, to the *Enûma Elish* of the Babylonians, we will recall that different gods are responsible for the formation of different animals. Since some of those gods are motivated by evil intentions, the

---

[61] Genesis 1:24–31.

product of their work can be understood to represent an expression of evil. In the Genesis narrative, however, Elohim is the only one responsible for the things of the world, calling the cosmos and everything in it into being from the void: as the Christian philosophers would later say, "*ex nihilo*" or "*out of nothing.*" John makes this point explicitly in the prologue of his Gospel, when he says, "All came to be through him. Without him, not one thing came into being."[62] Thus, everything in creation bears the stamp of God's own goodness, and God can survey the whole of what he has made and declare, "Aaah! Very good!"

This includes humanity, whom, in the discourse on the sixth day, Elohim "creates" in a discrete act. Once again, we should remember that the term "creation" has a specific meaning rooted in Elohim's unique ability to think and will something other than himself—that is, to *love* something into being. For the first time, then, since the initial movement of creation on the first day, we see the use of the word *bara'* (בָּרָא), which implies a free and conscious choice—an *election*, so to speak—to make something. This is the term that now comes to describe God's action with respect to his choice to speak humanity into existence. He does not simply "form" us, "make" us, or "shape" us (*asah* = עָשָׂה) out of what he had already fashioned, but instead, "creates" us (*bara'* = בָּרָא) in a new and distinct act of Love.

By contrast, in the Babylonian *Enûma Elish*, humanity is formed out the blood of Qingu, or, in some versions of the story, from Tiamat herself. In either case, we are an abomination: miniature personifications of the life of an evil and chaotic power, proliferating itself even in its death—indeed, proliferating itself *as* death. Our struggles in this

---

[62] John 1:3.

world sustain the order of the heavens, where the gods might finally take their rest at our expense. For this reason, human beings come into existence, in the Babylonian myth, in the seventh eon, not on the sixth "day" (*yom* [יוֹם] = *warmth* or *comfort*). Our existence brings repose to the *gods*, and it does so on the foundation of *our* perpetual restlessness.

The Biblical account, however, shows human beings as the culmination of God's act of creation, where each stage in the process deepens God's outward movement—his self-outpouring. Humanity is not the necessary evil upon which God secures a peace meant only for himself, but the completely capricious expression of God's super-abounding Love. This is why God's language changes at the point at which he turns to the creation of humanity. Now, rather than saying, "Let there be," commanding the appearance of whatever it is he seeks to bring into being, he says, instead, "let us accomplish-the-mighty-act" (*na'ăśeh* = נַעֲשֶׂה).

God involves himself directly in the creation of humanity, forming us, "in his own image: in the image of Elohim." This is a critical moment in the discourse, for it provides the whole basis of the biblical understanding of the meaning and value of the human person. We had already seen, in the discourse on the fourth day, that God formed the cosmos with human beings in mind, making the celestial bodies as a means of bringing the warmth and light of his love to our abode upon the earth. Now we come to the description of God's action in creating human beings, and we see that we ourselves now radicalize that same trajectory.

In human beings, God has made a creature to participate in, and to give expression to, the logic of the inner life of Elohim: the eternal dynamism of interpersonal love. This is the significance of God's words, "Let us accomplish-the-mighty-act." Here Elohim expresses his plural identity as it comes to bear upon his intentions in creating humanity. "Let us accomplish-the-mighty-act [of] humanity in our image: according to our likeness."

Not all scholars agree with this interpretation of the plural language of the narrative. Some see this language in Elohim's proclamation as an indication of a primitive polytheism reasserting itself in the context of this discourse. But we have already addressed this issue, saying that such a view cannot be supported in light of the purpose that, quite obviously, originally governed the construction of this whole narrative. The Hebrew people intended to articulate an entirely different worldview from that embraced by their former captors in Babylon. Its basis was the dogma of creation, which depended entirely upon the belief in an absolutely transcendent God who stands as the source of everything else there is, and who can think and will something other than himself. Given that this is the whole purpose of the narrative in question, any suggestion that the authors permitted a residual polytheism to creep into their narrative, especially at so critical a moment as the creation of human beings, is completely implausible.

Other scholars suggest that the plural language employed in this passage is intended as an expression of God's majesty—as the "royal we." This interpretation is plausible, but it is also much more radical than those who propose it might wish it to be. Tendencies abound in contemporary scholarship to minimize the theological uniqueness of the biblical perspective. Many scholars presuppose that the Bible appears as a collection of textual elements that emerge within the context of a broad and multifaceted religious milieu, where hundreds of similar cults influenced one another and competed for dominance. There is some truth to this point of view, but it does not serve us well as point of engagement with the Bible as it finally stands for the People Israel. There can be no question that the biblical faith in Elohim is, indeed, distinct from all pagan alternatives, and the Bible exists in great measure to make this very point.

Thus, we should not permit scholars to apply a contemporary democratic and egalitarian lens to the language of the Bible when Elohim employs the "royal we" in his creation of humanity. Rather, we should ask ourselves what the "royal we" actually implies in its own context—in a world governed by kings. If we do that, we will no longer be able to dismiss the divine proclamation as a primitive expression of a God who lords it over humanity (once again, as so many pagan deities would have been understood to do in the ancient world), for that is not the inner logic that the language of the "royal we" is meant to express.

We should note that the "royal we" comes to be employed in the creation narrative only at the moment at which God creates humanity. The reason is clear: human beings alone, in creation, belong to his kingdom as citizens—as participants in God's own interests. The "royal we" is the language a king employs when he seeks to represent the whole people in his own person. It expresses the fact that the king binds himself to the people of his kingdom, and implicates himself in their welfare. To suggest that God employs the "royal we" in the creation of humanity, then, is to say that God unites himself to humanity, declares us citizens of heaven, and, taking part in our history, implicates himself in what becomes of us. This is the God who, over and over again in the course of the Bible, will "hear the cry of the poor":[63] the God who will identify

---

[63] Cf. Exodus 2:24, 3:7; Job 34:28; Sirach 4:1–6, 21:5.

himself with his people by name, "for all generations to come."[64]

So, with the understanding, then, of these two dimensions of the creation of humanity in the image of Elohim—namely, that Elohim is the inter-relational God of love who seeks to create a being like himself in this way, and that Elohim so identifies himself with this creature as to implicate himself in our welfare—the full dignity of humanity according to the biblical narrative finally becomes apparent. It is a dignity that applies equally to both men and women, or, more properly, to men and women precisely insofar as they belong to one another. Returning, once again, to the text of the discourse, we read, "Elohim created humanity in his [own] image; in the image of Elohim he created them: male and female he created them."

Pope John Paul II had said that this sense of the biblical narrative is the most profound meaning of the text.[65] In the wake of a western interpretive tradition that places the weight of the divine image squarely on the intellect, Pope John Paul II noticed, rightly, that the text does not mention the power of reason in any explicit way. The whole logic of the story from beginning to end hinges on the movement of interpersonal love. When the author describes, for the first time, what it means to say that God creates humanity in his own image, he does not say, "rational he created them," but "male and female he created them." Let us look again at the discourse, here, to see just how emphatically the authors make this point. As if to leave no room at all for any misunderstanding as concerns this matter, they write:

---

[64] Exodus 3:15b.

[65] John Paul II, Wednesday Audience (14 November 1979), § 3.

> Elohim said, "Let us accomplish-the-mighty-act [of] humanity in our image: according to our likeness. . . ." Elohim created humanity in his [own] image; in the image of Elohim he created them: male and female he created them.

The point in this emphasis is not to diminish the importance of intellect in the image of God in human beings—what theologians refer to in Latin as the *imago Dei*—but, instead, to correct a prejudice against the emotive and relational dimension of human life on the grounds of paganism's dualistic view of the universe. According to that view, as we have already said, women are seen as somehow defective or evil. The Babylonians certainly held this view, but the Hebrew people did not. The biblical narrative transcends the dualistic worldview of pagan Babylon and all its dark and pessimistic implications, because the biblical narrative represents a faith in Love. No longer must we rely upon opposition and dichotomization for an understanding of our world and our place in it. No longer must we pit one power against another and turn reason against emotion, spirit against matter, the gods against mortals, or the masculine against the feminine. Humanity is not a side-effect or mistake; and women are not evil.

Indeed, the biblical narrative constitutes, on this point, an explicit affirmation that the material world is good, and that the bodily structure and the sexual differentiation of humanity are manifestations of the divine hand in creation. We are not speaking merely of how clever God is to make human beings in this way, but of how profoundly loving he is to do so. Human sexual differentiation—which is the only sexual differentiation explicitly referenced in this narrative—is the means whereby God creates a being who, like himself, experiences his own mode of existence in and through the dynamism of interpersonal relationality.

Of course we are not the only "social being" in the world. We are making a stronger point than that. Rather, human beings are the only animals capable of self-donation, and that, because we are the only animals who enjoy genuine self-possession. We are masters of our own lives, aware of being ourselves over-against other selves. We live in the context of an ongoing dialogue that opens up to us even before we leave the womb and continues throughout the course of our lives. The great twentieth-century Hasidic philosopher and rabbi, Martin Buber, correctly sees all of human existence as bound up in this dialogue, which may or may not be "genuine" depending upon how we dispose ourselves within it. For him, the moral dimension of human conduct comes into view at precisely this moment—the moment at which we determine whether to give or to withhold, whether to receive or to appropriate, whether to see the other as a person or as a thing. Buber's thesis gives expression to the inner logic of the Judeo-Christian covenantal attitude.

In the Christian tradition, the interpersonal character of (if we may use a rather phenomenological mode of expression) *human-beingness* is expressed covenantally in and through the sacramental actions of the Church. Each sacrament initiates, restores, or deepens one's participation in the dialogue of interpersonal existence that reaches even beyond other human beings to the inner life of God. Even the sacrament of Unction, administered by the priest when the threat of death asserts itself in our lives, constitutes a promise to continue the dialogue even beyond the horizon of the unseen. It is the Church's reassertion of Christ's promise that, in his triumph over death, our engagement in the dialogue of interpersonal existence will never be cut off definitively for the faithful, but may even deepen beyond the veil.

Herein lies the distinctly human condition: we possess ourselves in such a way that we can also give ourselves to others. We are able to affirm the interests of others as our own, to implicate ourselves in other people's lives as an active movement, and not merely as a passive happening beyond our control. We are capable of entering willfully into the dynamism of giving and receiving that characterizes the inner life of Elohim. We are made "in the image of God;" we are made to exist as ourselves precisely in our love for the other.

Nowhere is this dynamic more perfectly expressed in human existence than in the relationship between husband and wife, when it is lived in holiness and virtue. Elohim is the God of Love—the God who *is* Love, and whose love is self-expanding. God, in his Love, reaches beyond himself, enlarging the sphere of his own self-outpouring in the inner plurality of the divine Persons. Through the act of creation, Elohim—the God who is Father, Son, and Spirit—extends the dialogue of love beyond himself, and opens out to another who, only under this condition, exists to be loved at all.

A similar movement occurs in the case of marital love. In their mutual dynamism of total interpersonal giving and receiving, husband and wife together open out beyond their own shared life, and expand the sphere of their love to include another who comes to exist precisely in connection to that movement. Nowhere else in human life does love transcend limitation in quite this way. After all else is said and done, it is for this reason that the Judeo-Christian tradition can never accept same-sex marriage, which, of its nature, can never open out from within to bring another person into being.

Everything is at stake in this issue. To accept same-sex marriage, or to deny that the potentially life-increasing husband-wife union is uniquely normative for human beings, means rejecting the most fundamental datum of divine revelation: that God is *Elohim*, and that we are made in his image. The Judeo-Christian tradition's uncompromising condemnation of homosexual acts rests precisely here. It has nothing to do with hatred, bigotry, or fear; rather, it stems from the need to confess that the world is founded on Love—that it comes into being at the hands of Elohim, who so radically transcends all limitation that his Love can reach beyond his own inner relationality and call into being, into the scope of his embrace, someone wholly and entirely new.

Same-sex marriage is not the only matter tied to the dogmatic import of the discourse on the creation of humanity in the Genesis narrative. We can include here, by the very same logic, the Judeo-Christian tradition's historically pro-life expectations for married couples. Until 1930, all Christian denominations agreed in condemning the use of artificial contraception and abortion. This prohibition extends as far back into the Judeo-Christian tradition as it is possible to look—long before the time of Christ. In the Judeo-Christian tradition, openness to children is openness to God, and the choice deliberately to close off the gates by which the sphere of our love might be expanded further is the choice to reject God's creative presence in the *between* of husband and wife. The question perpetually before us in this covenantal context is whether we will allow ourselves to be more fully created in the Love of Elohim, or else close ourselves to that Love and constrict our humanity.

So central is the relationship between Elohim's self-revelation and the self-expanding, generative love of holy matrimony that the Church has recognized from ancient times its necessary connection to the work of salvation, as a sacrament for the building up of the Kingdom of God. The Church sanctifies matrimony and safeguards it, relying upon this movement of love between a man and a woman for her own future, drawing from its fecundity all her priests and religious, who will, "proclaim the Lord to generations to come, his righteousness to a people yet unborn."[66] St. Paul goes so far as to say that the sacrament of matrimony is a symbol of the union between Christ and Church[67]—an analogy drawn from a powerful and persistent thread running through the whole of Scripture.

We must not fail to lay a heavy stress on this point, though we cannot undertake an analysis here of the relevant texts, as the texts we have before us now have given us quite enough to consider already. We should, instead, return to the central purpose of the Genesis narrative—to articulate a view of the universe expressive of faith in Elohim. The God of the Bible is neither self-enclosed nor confined to his own abode. His radical transcendence means that there are no other gods worthy of the title, and that no boundary constrains his movements. God can move wherever he wills, and can love as deeply and vulnerably as he chooses. Thus, while the pagan gods, limited as they are within the cosmic frame, turn only to one another within the sphere of the heavens, Elohim turns to us. He seeks a spouse in his creation, drawing humanity to himself, opening his heart to us, and claiming us as his Bride.

---

[66] Psalm 22:30.

[67] Ephesians 5:21–33.

We cannot begin to explore this issue in any depth at this time, so profoundly expansive an issue is it in the biblical literature. But we should note that the New Testament image of Christ the Bridegroom rests entirely on this foundation. Indeed, the Incarnation event takes its logic from precisely this point in the Genesis narrative. We have already mentioned John's reading of the Genesis narrative in the context of the Christ-event as it is interpreted in the pages of his own writings. Even were we to concentrate our focus on John's reading alone, however, we would find ourselves completely overwhelmed with work. So, for the sake of the project before us, we must limit ourselves to an observation. John sees, in the Genesis narrative, the movement of the divine into his creation, and, now in the context of his experience of Christ, has come to understand how radical that movement really is. God was not content merely to *create* humanity; he intended from the very start to become one with us.[68]

---

[68] Earlier, we referenced Joseph Ratzinger's assertion in his collection of homilies entitled, *'In the Beginning': A Catholic Understanding of the Story of Creation and the Fall* (30), where he articulated precisely this view, known to theologians as "the universal primacy of Christ". This position is not that of St. Augustine or St. Thomas Aquinas, who held that God only becomes a human being to save humanity from sin after an initial fall from grace. The Augustinian/Thomistic opinion has become the dominant position in western Christianity, but, while it is considered dogmatic by many Protestants, it has never been affirmed as a dogma in the Catholic Church, and neither St. Augustine nor St. Thomas held this view with any insistence, at all. St. Thomas, in fact, concedes that prior to the Fall into sin, human beings would have believed explicitly in the Incarnation (*Summa Theologiae* II-II.2.vii)— a statement that leaves a great deal of room for the universal primacy. While he recognizes that the preponderance of the Tradition favors the view that God would have become incarnate even had there not been sin, the point he is concerned about making in his own answer to the question is simply the difference between explicit statements of the

When we read, then, in the discourse on the sixth day, that God said, "Let us accomplish-the-mighty-act [of] humanity in our image: according to our likeness," we should experience the same utter astonishment that John experienced when he first came to see that Jesus Christ has, in himself, radicalized this text, revealing its prophetic dimension. Once we accept that Jesus Christ is the Incarnation of God himself—of one Person of the Godhead, Elohim—then we immediately see that this "Son of Man" is the one in whom Elohim definitively realizes the making of humanity in his own image. God has inserted himself into his creation in the Person of Jesus Christ, having made *Adam* (אָדָם) according to his likeness.

We will leave this point to the side, for the moment. We will have to return to it again, of course, when we consider the discourse on the seventh day. And, while there is no possibility of treating the matter as it merits, we need to accept that, without some reference to this mystery, a genuinely Christian understanding of the issues before us cannot be attained.

In the mean time, we should turn to the fourth and final point to be gleaned from the discourse on the sixth day: God is provident for his creatures. But even here, the text is richly

---

divine action given in Scripture and interpretations of what is implicit (*Summa Theologiae* III.1.iii). From the point of view of the Catholic Church, the question is considered open, theologically, and the faithful are perfectly free to hold either opinion. In defense of the universal primacy, however—again, that God would have become Incarnate even had there never been sin—we should note that it does, indeed, represent the dominant view of the Fathers of the first millennium, that it is still the prevailing view among the Christians of the eastern rites, and that it has always boasted adherents in the West as well, including, among the Mediaevals, St. Bonaventure and Bl. Duns Scotus, and among recent popes, Benedict XVI and his immediate predecessor, John Paul II.

worded, and paints a picture that helps us make sense out of the world of our experience. God expresses his providence both by giving human beings and the beasts of the earth the food they need to live, and by investing humanity with a share in his own authority.

These two dimensions of divine providence together form the frame within which the relationship between humanity and God, and humanity and the world, comes into view. And, once again, we are brought face-to-face with the God of the Bible, to behold his goodness and love. For he says, "Aaah! I have given!" Our popular translations do not do justice to this phrase, for they tend to lose the dimension of awe the authors intended to communicate in favor of a sober and almost sterile communication of data. The real proclamation being made in this passage is that God is a giver—that he supplies what we need in our daily lives, and lavishes us with his goodness at every turn.

This includes sharing with the creature who bears his own image some measure of the power of his creative love. We have already discussed how this comes to be expressed in the marital relationship between husband and wife as they participate directly in the self-expansive love of Elohim. But tied to that very idea in this discourse is God's explicit investment of humanity with a share in his own authority over the things he has made.

The translation we have offered here brings to light the profundity of the issue at stake in this passage. The text reads, "Be fruitful, become many, fill the earth, and subject it to your authority. Exercise dominion over the fish of the sea, the birds of the heavens—[over] every living thing that moves upon the earth." This passage, then, will have practical implications for us today, as we consider which social and political agendas to espouse from within a covenantal framework of life. Without in any way intending to reduce faith to politics (indeed, to do so would be to deny faith's most fundamental character), we can say, for example, that tendencies in environmental politics to marginalize humanity, or to homogenize our standing with respect to other beings in the world, or to subordinate our interests to "Nature" or "the environment" as a higher value, are simply incompatible with the message of the Bible.

The Genesis narrative, in other words, as it leads up to the discourse on the sixth day, simply leaves no room for an environmental ethic predicated upon the assumption that human beings are but one species among many, who are unique only in the restrictions to be imposed upon their conduct. Too often in the modern world, Christians and Jews allow themselves to be persuaded that imprinting our environment with our influence and bending it to suit our needs is something harmful in itself to the world, and an offense against what God—or "Nature"—has made. There are those in the environmental movements who would call us "specieists" for presuming to possess rights we would not recognize for the beasts, as some would be called "racists" for claiming rights for one group of human beings they would deny to another. There are still others in the environmental movement who would see any impact of the human creature on the environment as destruction, and promote a worldview in which *we ourselves* are viewed as a kind of cosmic cancer, or as a foreign body in the tissues of the earth, to be purged.

Such views are entirely pagan. They have no foundation in the Bible, and are to be rejected. The whole of creation is made by God as a gift of love for us. As such, it is to be cherished and cared for by us. But it is also to be used by us and shaped by us, and "subjected to our authority;" for it belongs to us and is ordained by God to our welfare. We are not a mistake; we are not an unintended consequence, and we are not a necessary evil. We are the culmination of creation at the hands of Elohim; we are the manifestation of his love in the material world.

Day Seven

In our analysis of the discourse on the sixth day, we considered the importance of the meaning of the number six as an indication of "near fulfillment." We said that, according to the Jewish numerological tradition of gematria, the sixth day already calls out for a seventh, without which the meaning of creation remains a conundrum, for it would mean that the world remains unfulfilled. This condition cannot be perpetual without returning us to a fundamentally pagan perspective on the mystery of the universe. In fact, John makes exactly this point when he makes it the basis of "the number of the beast": 666.[69]

Scholars generally agree that the number of the beast is a numerological code for the name of Nero, who, as Emperor of Rome had engaged in a ruthless campaign of persecution against Christians. We do not contest that analysis at all, but we would suggest that John has another important meaning in mind as well. The number 666 is a number indicative of absolute frustration—a number that means *damnation*. The "beast" is supremely frustrated because he is forever unfulfilled. So close to perfection that he might be mistaken for God in the eyes of those who do not know God personally in Jesus Christ, he is really only a creature who

---

[69] Revelation 13:18

limits himself by rejecting the infinitely expansive love of Elohim. This self-constricting creature is depicted, in the book of Revelation as the spawn and vicar of, "that ancient serpent, the one called 'devil,' or the 'Satan,' the one who leads the whole inhabited world astray."[70] It, therefore, represents, once again, in this new context, that futile alternative—*any* alternative—to covenant with Yahweh Elohim. Indeed, the word, in this passage, that we translate, "the whole inhabited world," is *oikoumenein* (οἰκουμένην), which, in its common usage at the time referred to the Empire. For John to employ this term here is for him to say that the world of human beings, but, in particular, the pagan and secular Roman Empire, suffers from a tragic blindness that only faith in Jesus Christ can heal. The people of the Empire live in a world without God, and, for that reason, believe only in the limited powers of the present world, chief among which is Death.

The sixth day of creation, therefore, requires the seventh by the logic of *gematria*. Without fulfillment, it can only be damnation, because it will remain merely *other* than God, forever alienated from him, and drifting, therefore, further and further away from Eternal Love and Life.

This idea is central to the biblical perspective of creation at the hands of the God who is Love. Christianity, in fact, sees in Jesus Christ a total radicalization of this point; for Jesus Christ represents in his own person the moment in which creation returns to God definitively. The concept of

---

[70] Revelation 12:9. In Chapter 13, the dragon bequeaths "its power to act, its throne, and its great authority stemming from its own being" (cf. 13:2) to the beast, who rises from the abyss (13:1). The dragon is clearly the primordial goddess of the abyss, Tiamat of the *Enûma Elish*, which is why Rome now takes on the identity of Babylon (14:8).

the Sabbath day as it is understood in the Judeo-Christian context, expresses this intuition—that creation does not reach its fulfillment as long as it remains just what it is. It must move beyond itself, returning to the source of all Love—to the heart of Elohim.

So, here again, as we can see very clearly in the discourse on the seventh day, the Judeo-Christian tradition is completely different from paganism. In the *Enûma Elish*, the seventh eon saw the formation of human beings, that they might be pressed into the service of the gods, that the gods, in turn, might rest as humanity suffers the pains of toil, conflict, fear, and sorrow. The restlessness of humanity is the precondition for the repose of the gods, according to the *Enûma Elish*.

This is not the case at all in the biblical narrative, where God relates his own divine repose directly to the repose of his creation—to the repose of humanity. In the New Testament, Christ reminds us of this essential truth about the Sabbath day as it relates to the self-revelation of God. "The Sabbath came into being for humanity," he says, "not humanity for the Sabbath."[71] Christ means to say that the Sabbath is a gift of God to human beings for our fulfillment, not a means by which God extracts from humanity some necessary service. God does not need humanity, he desires us—he desires to love us, and to be loved by us. The Sabbath day stands for that divine intention. It tells us the whole purpose behind creation—a purpose we can only come to perceive because God has first revealed it to us. It tells us that God creates the world for humanity, and that he creates humanity because he seeks to invite us into his own inner life. This is why the Sabbath day, which represents this

---

[71] Mark 2:27.

divine intention, corresponds, in the Genesis narrative, to the *seventh* day—the day of "fulfillment." Turning, now, to the discourse on the seventh day, we offer the following translation:

> The heavens and the earth and all their hosts were completed. On the seventh day, Elohim completed his work which he had done. He rested on the seventh day from all the work which he had done. Elohim blessed the seventh day and made it holy, because Elohim took Shabbat from the whole of his labor, [with all] that he had created and shaped. These are the begettings of the heavens and the earth [when they] were created.[72]

One difficulty in translating this passage rests in the rather confusing phrases at the beginning of it. God brings no new entities into being on the seventh day, so the phrases we have translated here as "The heavens and the earth and all their hosts were completed. On the seventh day, Elohim completed his work which he had done," read like an editorial mistake. We have also opted to say that God, "took Shabbat from the whole of his labor," on the seventh day. We have done this better to reflect the etymological relationship between the words, *sheh'bah* (שֶׁבַע), *shabath'* (שָׁבַת), and *shabbath* (שַׁבָּת). *Sheh'bah* is the word for the number seven, *shabath'* means something like *rest, desist*, or *complete*, and *shabbath* is the word we transliterate as *Sabbath*: the religious observance. These concepts are all bound-up together in the Hebrew language, because they are all bound up with the biblical understanding of creation.

With these details in mind, then, we would like to suggest that the text of the discourse on the seventh day might be translated more freely as follows:

---

[72] Genesis 2:1–4a.

> The heavens and the earth and all their hosts were completed. But on the seventh day, Elohim brought to fulfillment the work he had done; he rested on the seventh day from all the work he had done. Elohim blessed the seventh day and made it holy, because, in the company of the whole of what he had created and shaped, he took Shabbat from all of his labor. *This* is how we ought to understand the bringing-forth of the heavens and the earth: that they were *created*.[73]

The hope expressed in this discourse is astonishing. Indeed, it is wholly new to the religious sensibilities of the ancient world. But what is the inner logic at work in this bizarre perspective? Why would anyone ever imagine that a God so radically transcendent as the Hebrew people suppose their God to be would, or even could, be, at the same time, a God of intimacy and nearness? Are not the two modes of existence mutually exclusive?

The Hebrew people understood, however, that the movement of creation could not terminate in the sheer *otherness* of the creature relative to God. Indeed, the horizon of the Sabbath rest is visible already by the light God brings into being on the first day. If we recall that, "Elohim called the light, 'day,' and the darkness he called, 'night'"—that he called the light, "warmth" or "comfort," and the darkness, "a twisting-away," then we can already see that his creation can only remain "good" insofar as it is able to return to him. If his creation moves out from him only, then it is "darkness": it is "a twisting away," and, therefore, something evil. Thus, if God's creation is to remain "light," it must make a return from sheer *otherness*, and find its way back to its source in the inner life of God.

---

[73] Genesis 2:1–4.

In the Middle Ages, theologians expressed this truth in terms of *"exitus"* and *"reditus"*—that is to say, "going-out-from" and "returning-to" God. They held that the movement of creation was circular rather than strictly linear—and that it was precisely for this reason that *history* was *not* circular, as it appears to be when viewed through pagan eyes. In the pagan religions, the world cycles endlessly over upon itself, each successive generation repeating precisely the same course as all the rest that had come before.[74] This presupposition lies at the heart of common pagan cults pertaining to the seasons of the year or the cycle of the moon, or to the idea of a "circle of life," whereby one generation lives on the condition that another one dies. Even theories about reincarnation ultimately reflect this fundamentally circular understanding of time.

The Judeo-Christian understanding of time, however, involves a clear trajectory of development. The thesis of the *exitus–reditus* dialectic—the movement out-from God and back-to God—replaces the perception of an enclosed circularity of the finite with the self-transcending circularity of infinite Love. Time does not repeat itself in this sort of a

---

[74] In the book of Ecclesiastes, Qoheleth gives expression precisely to this pagan point of view. His purpose is to present a picture of the world through pagan eyes—a portrait of a world without Yahweh Elohim as its source and Sabbath rest. This is the key to understanding that book in the biblical context; Qoheleth is not suggesting that the world really is a place of absolute futility, but that it *would* be if the pagans were right in the way they see the world. "What was will be again," he writes, "what has been done will be done again; and there is nothing new under the sun. Take anything of which it may be said, 'Look now, this is new.' Already, long before now, it existed. Only no memory remains of earlier times, just as in times to come next year itself will not be remembered" (Ecclesiastes 1:9–11). We quote here from *The Jerusalem Bible,* Reader's Edition, Alexander Jones, ed. (New York: Doubleday, 2000).

world, because it is wholly taken up into the unique and unrepeatable dynamism of Eternity, and, in that way, moved beyond itself by the divine hand.

Everything about this idea points in the direction of the Sabbath day. If we recall what we had said earlier about the pattern of the creation narrative—namely, that the week is divided into two sets of three that reflect one another, with the seventh day transcending the boundaries of time indicated by this structure—it will be easy to see that the Sabbath day represents the point at which the world of creation breaks beyond its own finitude to embrace its source in the Infinite. The authors communicate this meaning by dropping from the discourse on the seventh day the repetitive device with which the discourses on each of the previous days had been concluded: "evening fell and morning broke." The Sabbath day does not include this phrase because the Sabbath does not exist within time. Time, instead, exists within the Sabbath.

The creation of humanity on the sixth day, then, represents that point at which creation becomes capable of its return, God having created a being like himself, capable of self-transcending love, and, therefore, dialogue with Elohim. This is why the creation narrative cannot conclude with the creation of humanity alone, and why the creation of humanity must be situated on "the sixth day": the day of "near-completion." The *fulfillment* comes, not in humanity's mere existence, but in our actual return to God; but this movement can only happen when God becomes present to his creation—when he opens his heart to us and lets us in, taking us up into the eternal dynamism of his own inner Life. The Sabbath day means that creation is not in vain, that, in the end, whatever may happen in the interim, what God has made cannot finally and irrevocably "twist-away," from him, but will remain "light," because "his love is everlasting."[75] This is why the authors insist as they do upon telling *this* story not that they think it to represent a scientific account, as if such an account could even have been imagined within the context of that culture, but because *this* was a story about *creation*: the generation of the cosmos out of nothing but the love of Elohim, who thinks and wills the other into being. "*This*," the ancient priests confess, "is how we ought to understand the bringing-forth of the heavens and the earth: that they were *created*."

---

[75] Cf., for example, the Psalms alone on this point: 100, 103, 106, 107, 117, 118, and 136.

CHAPTER 5

ஐ

The Genesis Narrative After the Fall of Babylon

The Second Book of Maccabees contains a story relating to a mandate by the ancient king, Antiochus IV Epiphanes, who sought to eradicate the faith of Israel through force of law.[76] Recognizing that the real power of the faith lies in its ability to shape and bind the

---

[76] These events, which included what historians refer to as the Maccabean Revolt, occurred between 175–134 BC, and are the subject of the Septuagint books of 1–4 Maccabees. The Septuagint is the Greek Old Testament, which includes several books and narratives that do not appear in Hebrew. Many of these texts are accepted as canonical in the Catholic Church and in the apostolic churches of the

consciences of its adherents by virtue of its claim on truth, the attack on conscience and the attack on the truth-claims of Judaism formed, as it were, a "seamless garment" of persecution under his regime—a regime so brutal as to warrant legitimate comparison to the Nazi holocaust of the Second World War.[77]

This episode of history is worth our attention, because it illustrates the perpetual challenge that stands behind the whole of the Bible—to accept or reject the affirmation of a world founded on Love: a world that stands as the product of creation at the hands of a God who can think and will something other than himself. The light of divine revelation—the light of the Gospel—is, fundamentally, a proposal to the human person to accept this truth in all its implications, and be transformed by it. This truth is as vital today as it was at the time of the Babylonian exile, and at the time of Antiochus IV, centuries later. As we will see, faith in

---

East. The Catholic Church accepts the first two books of Maccabees as canonical, along with a number of other Septuagint-exclusive texts. The New Testament authors quoted from the Septuagint regularly, and appeared to regard the text as something more than a mere translation.

[77] Antiochus outlawed virtually every distinguishing mark of Judaism, making circumcision a capital offense for both children and their families (1 Maccabees 1:60–61), and forcing Jews under threat of death to violate the dietary rubrics of the Kosher laws and eat pork. In these gestures, Antiochus presumed to banish the God of the Covenant—to subject Elohim to the authority of an earthly king, and thus, to codify in law the practical renunciation of the Faith. Faced with the fundamental option proposed in the pages of Scripture—for a world limited within the horizons of this life, hemmed in by death, or a world of unbounded life in Covenant with the God who is Love, the Jewish people eventually staged a rebellion against the secular king.

Elohim and faith in creation amount to the very same stance—the one cannot stand without the other.[78]

Among Antiochus' offenses, was a positive mandate to eat pork. The response this mandate receives in the story of the woman and her seven sons in 2 Maccabees,[79] illustrates our point, explicitly. In that account, Antiochus found the woman and each of her seven sons absolutely intractable. Even in this seemingly superficial act,[80] they were completely unwilling to turn away from the God who loved the world into being. The story exists to make this point, complete with explicit references to the Genesis narrative we have been studying in the pages of this book.

---

[78] Because the logic of "creation" in the proper sense requires the affirmation that God freely wills his creature into being, it would be absurd to suggest in any strict sense that God *must* create. The relevant issue here is not what God *must* do, but what, in fact, he *does* do. Indeed, there could be no faith in Elohim without a created person to *have* faith; no one would exist to believe in Elohim and to trust in him, unless, in fact, Elohim created. Thus, faith in Elohim is faith in creation, and faith in creation is faith in Elohim.

[79] 2 Maccabees 7:1–42.

[80] We should keep in mind that the Jewish people do not see keeping Kosher as the thing that saves them. They understand it as a witness, representing their readiness to forego any convenience rather than forget about God, to whom the human person must be responsible in every moment. In the end, all the dietary restrictions and ritual actions of the rabbinical law are designed with this idea in mind: to keep our relationship with Elohim—the God of Love—ever in view. The point is to remember God at every turn, with every step and every breath, with every bite of food and every word we speak. When Paul says, "pray without ceasing," (1 Thessalonians 5:17), he has in mind this very sort of devotion, even if he has made concessions with respect to the exterior observances. For it is that interior conversion—the conformity of the human heart to the heart of God—which constitutes the real essence of the Torah that can never be abrogated.

The Woman and Her Seven Sons

The *seven sons* of the Maccabean narrative present a parallel to the seven *days* in the story of creation, and the mother provides, in the context of the story in 2 Maccabees, two explicit discourses on the mystery of *creation*. Here, unquestionably, the mother in this story represents Israel as the Bride of God, while the seven sons represent the faithful of all ages, who are born of her, and are faced at every moment and in every age, with the challenge to believe or not believe. This challenge falls to each one of us, all the way to the end of days, when history itself is transcended in the True Sabbath—"the day of mercy."[81]

The discourse following the death of the sixth son, therefore, must be read in light of the sixth day of the Genesis narrative, on which God makes human beings in his own image. This first maternal discourse is placed at this point in the narrative, but it is represented as a proclamation made to the whole group of her sons—to every heir of the Abrahamic Faith across the whole of time. She exhorts her sons, saying:

> I do not know how you appeared in my belly; it was not I who endowed you with spirit and true-life, nor had I the shaping of your every part. Therefore, [it is] the creator of the cosmos, shaping the coming-into-being of humankind, and presiding over the origins of all things, and who, assuredly, will give you back

---

[81] The literary placement of the mother's discourses is significant. The first is situated after the death of the sixth son, and the other before the death of the seventh. The seventh son, for his own part, offers a discourse involving a declaration of hope for the universalization of faith in the God of Israel, when all enmity will be overcome by love.

redoundingly both spirit and true-life in mercy, as now you disregard yourselves for the sake of his law.[82]

In her second discourse, which is directed to the seventh son—the son who represents the fulfillment of creation in the return of humanity to God in Sabbath rest, she recalls, once again, the mystery of creation. Exhorting her son in no uncertain terms, the Mother of the faithful begs her son to share her own confession of faith, saying:

> I beg of you, my child, behold heaven and earth, and consider all that is in them; know that God made them-to-be out of what did not exist, and that the human-being comes-into-being by such becoming. Do not be horrified by this torturer, but become worthy of your brothers: receive the death, so that, in the [day of] mercy, I may come-to-have you back in your brothers' company.[83]

Here we see that faith in Elohim *is* faith in creation, which means faith that the world is founded on Love and that life is stronger than death. This faith—what Pope John Paul II called "the gospel of life"—allows our consciences absolute freedom in the face of any threat. If the world is founded on Love, then there is no positive power of evil, and life will always have the final say. God has divided the abyss, he has "separated the light from the darkness," and "the light shines in the darkness, and the darkness did not constrain it."

---

[82] 2 Maccabees 7:22–23.

[83] 2 Maccabees 7:28–29.

Whither the Babylonians?

By this point in history, of course, the Babylonians had already gone extinct. And by the time Jesus preached the Gospel, no one had seen a Babylonian for nearly two-hundred years. After all their achievements over the course of the preceding centuries, immense and far-reaching as they were, their cultural influence had now been reduced to little more than traces and shadows surviving only in the cultures that had absorbed their dispersed descendents. The irony of this fact would not have been lost on the ancient Hebrew people: that the once-mighty Babylonians, who had held the Hebrew people in captivity, nearly driving them into oblivion themselves, would have Israel to thank today for their perpetual imprint on the history of the world. More than in any other way, the Babylonians survive today in the consciousness of their own captives—as a memory of Zion.

Why, then, do we even care about them now? Why, in God's infinite wisdom, does their own religious perspective feature so prominently in the Genesis narrative of the Bible, which is supposed to be relevant to all people of faith at all times and in every permutation of culture? If no one still holds the point of view the authors were trying to correct, why do we still need to read this narrative now?

The story of the woman and her seven sons in 2 Maccabees provides the answer to these questions. The real center of the problem in the Genesis narrative is not the Babylonian myth of origins itself, but what it represents as an alternative to faith in Elohim. For the ancient Hebrew people, this faith was seen, and rightly so, as the only thing of its kind, against which stood absolutely everything else—every other point of view humanity could ever embrace about the world. Either the world is founded on Love—

either *Elohim*—or not. Thus, even after the Babylonians had been extinct for centuries, John refers to them in the Book of Revelation. There, they come to stand for the secular power of Rome,[84] derived, ultimately, from, "that ancient serpent, the one called 'devil,' or the 'Satan',", who leads the Empire astray.[85] As we have already explained, this great dragon is intimately related to the image of the abyss, out of which the "Beast" arises, as if spawned, to assume the authority and power of the serpent and make its presence felt in the world of human beings.[86] There can be no question that Zion's memory of Babylon still survives in John's consciousness, and that what their worldview meant as an alternative to faith in Elohim still speaks to people of faith, even toward the close of the first century AD.

The fact that John's concern is not with an overtly religious enemy, but with a secular one, speaks directly to the question of the text's enduring relevance. From a political point of view, Rome was not like Babylon at all, since it did not legislate on the basis of any preconceived cultic commitments but on the basis of a purely secular preoccupation. In this respect, Rome bore a closer resemblance to a modern secular democracy than to most other political organisms of the time. John refers to Rome as *Babylon*, therefore, not because Rome embraces a specific cult, but because Rome does *not* embrace the cult of Elohim, and, instead, sets itself in opposition to that cult's definitive realization in the Covenant of Jesus Christ.

Pagans of all sorts have always existed alongside Israel and the Church; and, in all times, God's people have faced

---

[84] Revelation 14:8.

[85] Revelation 12:9.

[86] Revelation 13:1–2.

the same fundamental choice on their account—to affirm a world founded on love or something else instead. In the other direction, the people of God have always offered humanity a different way—a way out of the darkness and into the light. No matter what the particulars, the basic thrust of the Genesis narrative remains the same. If the world is founded on Love—if God is Love—then the world is good, humanity exists for love, and life is worth living. This truth remains, even if the culture we are encountering is a totally atheistic one.

The Modern Areopagus

In our time, the Judeo-Christian tradition is a world-wide religious presence. Jews are spread far and wide, while Christians live in every nation on earth. It is difficult for us to appreciate, today, just how radical the Judeo-Christian perspective really is, because it has been so profoundly transformative as a world-wide cultural force that not a single developed nation on the planet has entirely escaped its moral influence. Even nations that remain culturally pagan now take for granted one or another decidedly Judeo-Christian moral precept—typically very many of them—without even realizing it. Pope John Paul II had seen this state of affairs in hopeful terms, saying:

> If the world is not Catholic from a denominational point of view, it is nonetheless profoundly permeated by the Gospel. We can

even say that the mystery of the Church, the Body of Christ, is in some way invisibly present in it.[87]

Of course he was right in finding hope in this fact, but he also understood that it leaves the gospel subject, paradoxically, to new vulnerabilities, calling the Church to a new challenge—a "new evangelization." If we do not realize that the values we hold dear belong to the Judeo-Christian tradition, and not to philosophical inquiry alone, much less to science or technology, then we will not understand what is at stake in abandoning that foundation. We will undermine those very values by cutting down the Tree or uprooting the Vine that bears them as its fruit. In this way, even the well-intentioned can become complicit in advancing an agenda that will finally work against the interests of humanity.

When the Constitution of the European Union was adopted in June of 2004, Pope John Paul II criticized the document markedly for its omission of any mention of modern European culture's Christian origins, even after extended pleas from the Vatican. As a fact of history, modern Europe *is* a product of Christianity, even if the twentieth century was marked by the gradual emergence of a cultural consensus to abandon its own historical foundations. The Catholic Church wanted to see the European Union at least acknowledge the actual historical fact of Europe's Christian heritage, because she understood that many of Europe's distinguishing moral characteristics actually stem from that heritage, and that abandoning that heritage means, in the long term, abandoning the values that set her apart from the rest of the world as a humane society. The actual

---

[87] John Paul II, *Crossing the Threshold of Hope*, Vittorio Messori, ed., Jenny McPhee and Martha McPhee, trans. (New York: Alfred A. Knopf, 1994), 112.

language finally adopted by the Constitutional Committee reads as follows:

> [The European Union draws its] inspiration from the cultural, religious and humanist inheritance of Europe, from which have developed the universal values of the inviolable and inalienable rights of the human person, democracy, equality, freedom and the rule of law.

Anyone who really understands intellectual history can readily see that the Catholic Church is right in its basic criticism here, and that there is no room at all for a debate about the facts. The general acknowledgment of a "religious" inheritance right alongside a vaguely "humanist" inheritance is not nearly specific enough to account for Europe's embrace of "the inviolable and inalienable rights of the human person" as a "universal value." Such a concept comes only from the Judeo-Christian tradition, and nowhere else. Indeed, the idea of "person" itself—apart even from any question of "inviolability" or "inalienable rights"—belongs entirely to the Judeo-Christian tradition. It is *not* a product of philosophical inquiry at all, but a contribution *to* philosophy by the Fathers of the Church, as they developed language within which to express the Trinitarian inner structure of Elohim—the God of the Bible, who is plural in his unity. It is on this basis that "personhood" is first understood in terms of "inviolability." Thus, the consciousness of a truly "inviolable" dignity for the human being finds its way into the philosophical dialogue only once the language of "personhood" comes to be applied, in a secondary way, to human beings on account of the revealed truth that we are made by Elohim "in his own image: according to his likeness." It is simply naïve to suggest, today, that the concept of "the inviolable and inalienable rights of the human person" is a "universal value." It is not; it is a distinctly Judeo-Christian value: a conclusion drawn from concerted theological reflection on the God of the Bible.

The fact that the framers of the European Union's Constitution could not understand or even perceive this fact tells us that the story of creation in the Genesis narrative is as relevant today as it was when it was first composed. The People of God still need this narrative, even though the context within which we receive it is very different on the surface. Today's Babylon is not a polytheistic paganism steeped in mythology and primitive superstitions; it is a generally atheistic secularism steeped in the mythology of quantification and a superstitious confidence that natural science can transform the world of our experience into a utopia.

Today's Babylon, in other words, is the deceptive seduction to the idea that humanity has evolved beyond the need for religion—beyond the need for God. We find this attitude reflected everywhere in modernity. Today, in Europe and the United States, society is increasingly embracing the idea that scientific and technical knowledge can supplant religion, even as a basis for morality, and that the Judeo-Christian tradition stands, not as the foundation of a culture of human dignity, but as a barrier to that culture's maturity, and as an obstacle to personal liberty. This point of view is based upon an ignorance of history, and it can only lead, as it has in every instance in which it has been promoted in the course of the past hundred years and more, to a diminishment of human dignity—to a trampling of, "the inviolable and inalienable rights of the human person." This is not a debatable point; for we have replayed this drama countless times, only to see it end the very same way on each occasion.

Still, we find ourselves always fighting the same battle, and this is the point of the Genesis narrative, no matter the particulars of the opposition. Whether in reply to the culture of ancient Babylon or modern Berkeley (or any one of hundreds of other university campuses throughout the western world), whether in reply to a procurator of ancient Rome or a bureaucrat of today's Federal Government, to an ancient Emperor or a modern President, the fundamental conversation is the same. The question of human existence is always the same, and what we say about God and Creation means everything in the formation of our answer. Pope John Paul II saw, in the Church's call to a "new evangelization," the need to fight a "culture war" on this very front, where, again, the new Babylon is not a pagan mythos but a pervading secularism propounded by the "intelligentsia" of our age. He writes:

> Against the spirit of the world, the Church takes up anew each day a struggle that is none other than *the struggle for the world's soul*. If in fact, on the one hand, the Gospel and evangelization are present in this world, on the other, there is also present *a powerful anti-evangelization* which is well organized and has the means to vigorously oppose the Gospel and evangelization. The struggle for the soul of the contemporary world is at its height where the spirit of this world seems strongest. In this sense the encyclical *Redemptoris Missio*[88] speaks of *modern Areopagi*. Today these *Areopagi* are the worlds of science, culture, and media; these are the worlds of writers and artists, the worlds where the intellectual elite are formed.[89]

---

[88] Pope John Paul II is referring here to his encyclical of 7 December 1990. The relevant passages in the encyclical are §§ 37.c–38.

[89] John Paul II, *Crossing the Threshold of Hope*, 112–113.

The real issue is always the same, no matter what the outward shape of the tension. It is the fundamental question at the heart of the Bible—whether the world is founded on Love or on something else instead: whether "In the beginning, Elohim created," or not.[90]

The Irony of Modernity

The question about Elohim and Creation arises anew in our own time because, today, people desire to be "free" in a radical, and historically unprecedented sense. In the modern world, we tend to see personal autonomy as the one universally binding moral norm. According to the general consensus of the broader philosophical dialogue, and the general sense we have as human beings, cross-culturally, we understand ourselves to possess the power to choose between alternative courses of conduct. That much is nothing new. The modern human being goes beyond this consensus, however, affirming that we possess a positive right to engage in whatever course of conduct we desire,

---

[90] The mandate from the Department of Health and Human Services in the United States in 2012, that the Church provide funding for artificial contraception, abortion, and sterilizing mutilation procedures, proceeds from this "modern Areopagus" as it propounds "the wisdom of the world" (1 Corinthians 3:19), and "of this age" (1 Corinthians 2:6), according to which the Church is an enemy of progress, and needs to be corrected as to the content of the Gospel and the meaning and structure of love. Once more in the present age, the Church is being told by a secular power that secular interests have the final moral say. By "throwing down the gauntlet" over artificial contraception and abortion, Secretary Sebelius has placed President Barack Obama in the position of Antiochus IV, advancing the prerogatives of a secular power by crushing the religiously-informed consciences of the faithful.

without regard to questions of what is conventionally "right" or "wrong," and without regard to what is strictly possible. For the modern human being, we possess a right to bend the very structure of reality and truth to conform to our own desires.

It is important for us to appreciate just how radical a departure from tradition modernity represents in this element. In previous ages, human beings understood that there were limits to human conduct dictated by the options placed naturally before us—that we could choose whether or not to eat, but not whether or not to starve in the absence of food, or that we could choose whether or not to marry, but not whether to be male or female. In our own age, however, all of this is changing, and advances in technology have been employed to justify this delusion. It comes, however, at a terrible cost: as a repudiation of the very foundation upon which rights claims of any kind can be advanced in the first place—the "image of Elohim" in the human person. On this new model, the sixth day *must* be the last day, and it cannot be a "day." There neither is nor ought to be a Sabbath, because the human individual exists for himself alone, and not for the other. There is no place in this sort of a world for the God of the Bible: a God who can say, "I have given!" And, for that reason, in the modern world, there is no human *person* in the proper sense, as a discovery of the Judeo-Christian tradition. Whether consciously or unconsciously, the one who opts for modern secularism is the "fool," who, "says, in his heart, 'there is no Elohim.'"[91]

The world that arises on this paradigm is a world without love, however full it might be of compassion and emotion. It is a world without hope, however full it might be of

---

[91] Psalms 14:1, 53:1.

aspiration and ambition. The modern human being lives in a world folded in upon itself, a world closed off to the infinite, bound mercilessly within the limits of time and space. For, the modern human being is forced to concede that, after he has lived out the whole of his self-directed life of individual choice, he remains, inescapably subject to the authority of death.

The irony, in other words, now undeniably clear, is that the modern human being rejects the very thing that makes what he seeks imaginable in the first place. He repudiates faith in Elohim and seeks to purge the God of the Bible from the whole horizon of human consciousness because he thinks that Elohim restricts his freedom. But, in this very move, the modern human being imprisons himself within a sphere of ruthless finitude from which Love alone can set us free. Only the God of the Bible—only Elohim—can share his inner life with us, constraining death itself, and dispelling the darkness of the abyss. Thus, Elohim is the only God who liberates us at all—not *from* the moral law, but *in and through* the moral law. The God of the Bible frees us from the oppressive threat of death, to live our moral principles without fear of what might happen if we love without reserve.

The Enduring Wisdom of the Dogma of Creation

In the Genesis narrative, we learn that human beings are made in the image of Elohim as male and female—that we can only be who and what we truly are insofar as we belong to the *other* and not merely to ourselves. The Genesis narrative thus teaches us that we can never be finally autonomous—that we can never be a "law unto ourselves," responsible to no one—because that is not what *God* is like.

From eternity and forever, God himself is Love. To be God is to be in conversation with the community: the Father with the Son in the Spirit, the Son with the Father in the Spirit, the Spirit of the Father and the Son. Because we are made in the image of *this* God, we are created into a similar mode of being—a mode of being analogous to that of Elohim. We are, whether we like it or not, referenced always to the other, not merely to ourselves, and we cannot, therefore, define our own existence simply as we like. Rather, the full realization of who we really are can only come in conversation with the whole—in a self-transcending, sacrificial love.

Love of this sort—what the authors of the New Testament call by the Greek word, *agapei* (ἀγάπη)—must, from the point of view of Faith in Elohim, constitute the real norm upon which any moral question before us will finally have to be resolved, for, as Christ reminds us, "on these two commandments the whole Law hangs, and the Prophets."[92] In the final analysis, with each choice we make in the course of our lives, we will have to ask whether the action we propose to undertake in the here and now is a move in the direction of self-transcending love or self-constriction—whether it opens or closes the human heart. We will have to ask whether we are choosing to love more fully, more expansively, and more vulnerably, or to limit the depth of our love, the sphere of our love, or the implications of our love. We will have to ask whether we are choosing the self at the expense of the other, or the other through the offering of the self.

Precisely in this observation, then, can we come to see, once again, where modernity has mistaken a shadow for reality; for we see, in the biblical norm of *agapei*, what

---

[92] Matthew 22:40. Cf., also, Galatians 5:14.

genuinely "free love" must really involve. It is not a self-satisfying exchange of favors with friends and strangers, no strings attached. Instead, it is the interweaving of the individual with the whole in the realm of responsibility and sacrifice. We are used to the sappy sentimentality that reduces the gospel to a call to "niceness" on the grounds that "God is Love,"[93] and that "God so loved the world that he sent his only-begotten Son,"[94] but we do not notice at all that the word in use in both instances here is *agapei*. God is "being-with", "belonging-to", and "being-for" the other, not an isolated Self apart from, and aloof from the concerns of others. And, in Jesus Christ, God enters into this sort of relationship with the cosmos, assuming obligations and taking responsibility in and through his choice to love us. The Bridegroom cannot take his Bride, on the model of the Gospel, without taking responsibility for her, and delighting in the fruitfulness of their embrace.

Creation or Evolution?

But it is precisely with this realization that we now return to the idea of evolution and modern science that we had taken up at the beginning of this book. Many Christians today, usually from the Evangelical traditions, but sometimes from the Catholic tradition as well, oppose the idea of evolution as somehow contradicting Scripture. We have already addressed this issue in a preliminary way. In our commentary about the language of the Genesis narrative as it concerns the formation of living things, we said that the

---

[93] 1 John 4:16.
[94] John 3:16.

authors employ language suggestive of material "biologization," or the self-organization of matter into biological forms by divine command. From a Christian point of view, then, suggestions of this sort should not disturb us. And, once again, we should remember that the Genesis narrative is not really concerned with the actual method and sequence by which God created, but with the meaning of the world *as* a product of creation—with advancing the utterly unique faith-conviction that the world is, in fact, created by God in an act of love.

Turning the tables, then, the Genesis narrative's model of material biologization, insofar as it presents a picture of what happens on the side of nature, is entirely consistent with modern evolutionary theory. If the modern scientist rejects the creation narrative, then, his opposition has nothing to do with anything the authors purposed to say about the material processes of biological organization. His problem rests with the idea of creation itself—with the idea of *Elohim*—which, in any event, is a question that lies totally outside his professional competency. His view about the God of the Bible is not a matter of scientific investigation, because the methods of natural science cannot approach this subject at all. Thus, the natural scientist must respond to the question of Elohim in exactly the same way as anyone else (as a human being, only, not as a scientist) and just as anyone else, he may take a stand of faith or not. Science has nothing to do with it.

When, again, we come to understand what is really at stake in the Genesis narrative, we realize that the defense of a purely propositional reading of the text, whereby we take as "literal" truth the precise method, sequence, and timeframe within which the world comes into existence in its present form, is a fool's errand. We are fighting a different battle than the one the authors of the narrative intended to fight. What is more, we are doing it for no good reason, and at the expense of the Bible's real message, and even its credibility.[95]

Indeed, we need to realize that the option to defend a strictly literal reading of the narrative of the seven days puts the Bible in the position of contradicting itself in the next chapter, when, in the garden narrative, a different sequence of events occurs. It is clear in the narrative of the seven days that vegetation comes into being on the third day, while animals emerge only on the fifth and sixth days, respectively, and human beings are the last to appear. But in the garden narrative, we read that God first forms the human being out of the dust of ground before he causes vegetation to spring up, "for Yahweh Elohim had not rained upon the earth, and there was no human being to cultivate the soil."[96] Once God does plant a garden and hand it over to the human being, however, he makes the beasts to be his servants. They are formed by God and brought before the man, who then

---

[95] We must admit, of course, that some of the Fathers did insist upon a literal reading, not unreflectively, but in the face of alternative interpretations. We do not at all intend to belittle them, but propose, instead, a way of understanding them in their own context. Ephraim the Syrian, to whom the Church cannot even begin to measure her debt, did not advance such a reading out of sheer ignorance or anti-intellectualism, but because the forces of Gnosticism running rampant in his day had come to appropriate many of the personalities and figures of the orthodox Faith into their own dualistic, neo-pagan systems of thought. His position is a reaction against the excessively abstract interpretations of the Genesis narrative reflected in the writings of the Gnostic sects, which stripped the narrative of its most fundamental meaning—that the world is loved into being by a God who thinks and wills something other than himself.

[96] Genesis 2:5.

names and dominates them.[97] There is no way around this problem: the sequence of the garden narrative and the sequence of the narrative of the seven days are different, so the insistence on propositional literalism in the case of one will mean denying propositional literalism in the case of the other, or else defending two contradictory positions simultaneously.

So the question arises, why we would feel the need to defend propositional literalism in either case, and on what criteria we would decide which of the two narratives to treat in this way. The tendency arises from a misguided belief that everything in the Bible must be literally factual in the "plain sense" because anything else would put God in the position of having made a mistake or having lied to humanity. But this approach to the Bible has nothing to do with the way in which the Bible was read by those who first received it. In fact, we have already considered in this very study how some of the human authors of the biblical texts themselves read other passages in Scripture in allegorical ways, and not as simple propositional assertions. Many of the Fathers of the Church understood both the narrative of the seven days and the garden narrative in allegorical terms, not as propositional reports of concrete facts to be interpreted literally. Barnabas the apostle, for example—the companion of Paul who features prominently in Acts—interprets the whole Genesis narrative in terms of the *Parousia*: Christ's return in the fulfillment of history. He writes:

> Notice, children, what he means by the words, "he completed them in six days." He means this: in six thousand years the Lord will make an end of all things; for, in his reckoning, the "day"

---

[97] Genesis 2:18–20.

means "a thousand years."⁹⁸ ... Therefore, children, in six days—in the course of six thousand years—all things will be brought to an end. "And he rested on the seventh day." This is the meaning: when his Son returns, he will put an end to the era of the Lawless One, judge the wicked, and change the sun, the moon, and the stars. Then, on the seventh day, he will properly rest.⁹⁹

This is only one example among many we could supply to the reader. The Fathers were not generally concerned with defending a strictly literal reading of the Bible, because they understood that God speaks to us through images and allegories, and not only in logical propositions. The apostles themselves attest to this fact when, after hearing Christ discourse at length about the mystery of salvation as they sat with him for the Last Supper, they finally identify a shift from allegory and parable to plain language.¹⁰⁰

It is fruitless, therefore, to fight the wrong battle and find, in the process, that we have taken up arms with only a tiny band of disoriented comrades while the whole army of Christendom is organized in a life-and-death struggle being waged on a different front. The real battle, as we have already said, is the battle for *meaning* and *value*. It is the

---

[98] MY FOOTNOTE: See Psalm 89:4 and 2 Peter 3:8.

[99] *The Epistle of Barnabas* 15:4–5. The translation here is that of James A. Kleist, with adaptations in formatting and punctuation to conform to the present manuscript. See, James A. Kleist, S.J., Ph.D., trans., *The Didache, The Epistle of Barnabas, The Epistles and Martyrdom of St. Polycarp, the Fragments of Papias, the Epistle to Diognetus*, Ancient Christian Writers: The Works of the Fathers in Translation, No. 6 (New York, N.Y./Mahwah, N.J.: The Newman Press: 1948), 37–65 (59).

[100] John 16:29. Christ had admitted earlier, in fact, that he had been speaking figuratively (John 16:29). We should not conclude, then, that he had been lying, nor that he had himself been deceived.

battle for the affirmation as established fact (even if it is a fact we can only know by revelation) that God is Love, that he thinks and wills something other than himself, that he loves the world into being for the sake of human beings, whom he makes in his own image. Our battle is the battle against the idea that the world is a randomly-emergent event with no intentional cause. It is the battle against the idea that the universe in which we live has no already-given-meaning, but only the meaning we assign it. Today's battle is the battle against the thesis that human beings are only one species among many, and that we appeared on the earth and survive today only because we were somehow better adapted to the cold and heartless reality of a universe founded on ruthless probabilities. Ours is the battle against those who say that human beings enjoy no privilege with respect to other beings in the world, and that the world might well exist without us, or might even be better off if it did.

Today's battle is not a battle for the literal propositional reading of the narrative of the seven days, but a battle for the inner motivating value behind its composition in the first place. It is a battle for the meaning behind the text—a battle for faith in Elohim, the God of Love, and the only God who could think and will something other than itself. It is the battle, not for a particular sequence or method of action on the part of God, but a battle for the underlying truth being revealed to us—that we are not a side-effect, an unintended consequence, an unfortunate outcome, a necessary evil, or a probability finally realized as so many countless trillions upon trillions of quantum particles randomly pulse away at material formations. Today's battle is the battle for the Bible's first and foundational affirmation: "In the beginning, Elohim created the heavens and the earth."

APPENDIX

༄

The Genesis Narrative in Translation

1 In the beginning, Elohim created the heavens and the earth. ²The earth was formless and void, and darkness overlaid the surface of *abyss*—and the Spirit of Elohim was moving-gently upon the face of the waters. ³Elohim said, "Let there be light," and there was light; ⁴Elohim saw that the light was good. And Elohim separated the light from the darkness. ⁵Elohim called the light, "day," and the darkness he called, "night." Evening fell and morning broke: day one.*

---

* FREE TRANSLATION: In the beginning, Elohim created the heavens and the earth. Rather than the earth, there was formlessness and void, and *abyss* was overlaid in darkness—and over-against this emptiness,

⁶Elohim said, "Let there be an expanse in the midst of the waters, [so] the waters become divided-between." ⁷Elohim made the expanse, and divided-between: between the waters which were beneath the expanse [and] the waters which were upon the expanse; and it was, just-so. ⁸Elohim proclaimed the expanse, "heavens." Evening fell and morning broke: day two.†

⁹Elohim said, "Let the waters beneath the heavens be detained in one area [and] the dryness show forth." And it was, just-so: ¹⁰Elohim proclaimed the dryness, "earth", and the gathering-together of the waters he proclaimed, "seas". And Elohim saw that it was good. ¹¹Elohim said, "Let the earth grow green with grass, with vegetation bearing seed, and with fruit trees developing fruit bearing seed for their own kind on the earth." And it was, just-so: ¹²the earth grew green with grass, with vegetation bearing seed, and with fruit trees developing fruit bearing seed for their own kind. Elohim saw that it was good. ¹³Evening fell and morning broke: day three.

¹⁴Elohim said, "Let there come to be lights in the partition of the heavens to divide-between: between the "day" and the "night." Let them come to be as indicators for festivals, days, and years. ¹⁵Let them come to be as lights in the partition of

---

the Spirit of Elohim moved-caressingly. Elohim said, "Let there be light," and there was light; Elohim saw that the *light* was *good*. And Elohim separated the *light* from the *darkness*. Elohim called the light, "warmth" or "comfort," and the darkness he called, "a twisting-away." Evening fell and morning broke: day one.

† FREE TRANSLATION: Elohim said, "Let there be, in the midst of the waters, a partition to come between them and divide them from within." Elohim made this partition, dividing the waters from within. It was just that way: a severance of the waters beneath the partition from the waters that rest upon the partition. Elohim proclaimed the partition, "heavens." Evening fell and morning broke: day two.

the heavens, to become-light upon the earth." And it was, just-so. ¹⁶Elohim made the two great lights—the greater light to govern the day, and the lesser light to govern the night—and the stars. ¹⁷Elohim placed them in the partition of the heavens to become-light upon the earth, ¹⁸to govern the day and the night, and to divide-between: the light from the darkness. Elohim saw that it was good. ¹⁹Evening fell and morning broke: day four.

²⁰Elohim said, "Let the waters teem with swarms of living things. Let birds fly above the earth, on the face of the partition of the heavens." ²¹Elohim made the great dragons, and every living thing that moves about, that swarmed the waters in their kind, and every kind of winged bird. Elohim saw that it was good. ²²Elohim blessed them, saying, "Be fruitful and become many. Fill the waters and the seas; birds, become many upon the earth." ²³Evening fell and morning broke: day five.

²⁴Elohim said, "Let there emerge from the earth living things by their kind: beasts and creeping things—[things] of the earth alive by their kind." And it was, just-so. ²⁵Elohim made the living of the earth by their kind: the beasts in their kind, and every species that creeps upon the ground.

²⁶Elohim said, "Let us accomplish-the-mighty-act [of] humanity in our image: according to our likeness. Let them have dominion over the fish of the sea, the birds of the heavens, all the beasts of the earth, and every creeping thing that creeps upon the earth."

> ²⁷Elohim created humanity in his [own] image;
> in the image of Elohim he created them:
> male and female he created them.

²⁸Elohim blessed them; Elohim said, "Be fruitful, become many, fill the earth, and subject it to your authority. Exercise

dominion over the fish of the sea, the birds of the heavens—[over] every living thing that moves upon the earth."

[29]Elohim said, "Aaah! I have given: all vegetation yielding seed that is on the face of the whole earth, and every tree that has fruit; every tree yielding seed shall become food. [30]For all the living of the earth—[for] every bird of the heavens and everything that creeps upon the earth that is a living thing—green herbs [are their] food." And it was, just-so. [31]Elohim saw all that he had made: "Aaah! Very good!" Evening fell and morning broke: the sixth day.

2 The heavens and the earth and all their hosts were completed. [2]On the seventh day, Elohim completed his work which he had done. He rested on the seventh day from all the work which he had done. [3]Elohim blessed the seventh day and made it holy, because Elohim took Shabbat from the whole of his labor, [with all] that he had created and shaped. [4]These are the begettings of the heavens and the earth [when they] were created.‡

---

‡ FREE TRANSLATION: The heavens and the earth and all their hosts were completed. But on the seventh day, Elohim brought to fulfillment the work he had done; he rested on the seventh day from all the work he had done. Elohim blessed the seventh day and made it holy, because, in the company of the whole of what he had created and shaped, he took Shabbat from all of his labor. *This* is how we ought to understand the bringing-forth of the heavens and the earth: that they were *created*.

Made in the USA
San Bernardino, CA
06 January 2014